Too
Awesome   June 29, 2022
↓

Carrie,
May God Always
Bless you and your
beautiful Family ♡
Love you So Much,
Kristin

Sunrise

Life after Traumatic Brain Injury:
A Healing Journey in Surviving TBI
An Empowering True Story

KRISTIN ABELLO

ARCHWAY
PUBLISHING

Archway Publishing books may be ordered through booksellers or by contacting:

Archway Publishing
1663 Liberty Drive
Bloomington, IN 47403
www.archwaypublishing.com
844-669-3957

Because of the dynamic nature of the Internet, any web addresses or links contained in this book may have changed since publication and may no longer be valid. The views expressed in this work are solely those of the author and do not necessarily reflect the views of the publisher, and the publisher hereby disclaims any responsibility for them.

Any people depicted in stock imagery provided by Getty Images are models, and such images are being used for illustrative purposes only. Certain stock imagery © Getty Images.

ISBN: 978-1-6657-1208-8 (sc)
ISBN: 978-1-6657-1209-5 (hc)
ISBN: 978-1-6657-1217-0 (e)

Library of Congress Control Number: 2021918868

Print information available on the last page.

Archway Publishing rev. date: 11/30/2021

To

Raul, thank you for always holding me tight
And being my forever. I love you.

My boys,

Jacob, My Powerful and Intelligent

Colin, My Clever and Insightful

Mom and Dad,

Viya and Buelo.

I love you forever.

Contents

Foreword

As reported by the Brain Injury Association of America, there are 3.5 million individuals and families who experience brain injury each year, with 61,000 related deaths in the United States in 2019. That is about 166 TBI-related deaths every day. The U.S. Centers for Disease Control and Prevention (CDC) recognizes traumatic brain injury (TBI) as a serious public health concern. Today at least 5.3 million Americans live with a TBI related disability.

According to the CDC, TBI is caused by a bump, blow, or jolt to the head that disrupts the normal function of the brain. Not all blows or jolts to the head result in a TBI. The severity of a TBI may range from "mild" (i.e., a brief change in mental status or consciousness) to "severe" (i.e., an extended period of unconsciousness or memory loss after the injury).

Most TBIs that occur each year are mild and commonly called concussions. Yet TBI causes a substantial number of deaths and leads to life-long disability for many Americans. The effects of a TBI can vary significantly, depending on the severity. Individuals with a mild TBI generally experience short-term symptoms and feel better within a couple of weeks, whereas individuals with a moderate or severe TBI may have long-term or life-long effects from the injury.

A severe TBI not only impacts the life of an individual and their family, but also has a large societal and economic toll. The lifetime economic cost of TBI, including direct and indirect medical costs, was estimated to be approximately $76.5 billion (in 2010 dollars).*

Source: Centers for Disease Control

Introduction

Dear Reader,

In 2002, while on a training run in Houston, Texas with my husband, Raul, in preparation for the Marine Corp Marathon to be held that year in Washington, DC, I was suddenly struck by a car. As a result, I sustained a traumatic brain injury, among other physical traumas.

This is my story of faith, love, hope, and healing from TBI. While a love story, it is also the true story of my fight for survival. My husband and I were a young couple in love when the catastrophic car accident nearly pulled us apart. In the end, faith, love, and courage united us more than ever.

My purpose in writing this memoir is to share my experience and to help survivors of catastrophic accidents and their families, friends, and caregiving communities. To give hope. This is a book I wish my husband and family had at the time to guide them, as there is life post brain injury or post any traumatic health experience. The complexity of our brains and the power of plasticity is nothing short of amazing.

I hope and pray that through my story, you will find strength, hope, and inspiration in overcoming your own hurdles. The common ground of perseverance will shine through.

Love,
Kristin

Prologue

Union Square

The psychic approached us. She was a pretty, young brunette in gray jeans and a black cardigan. Her lips spread in a bright smile as she asked if we wanted our palms read. My sister and I looked at one another, then back at the psychic. Sure, why not? It was just a little fun. The streets were busy, cars were zooming past. San Francisco was alive with the energy of either Stockton, Powell, or Geary in Union Square; I don't remember which, but it was most likely Stockton Street.

We followed the psychic to the steps of a building that could have been a courthouse or a library. This lighthearted fun was one more way to highlight the breezy, seventy-degree afternoon that was slightly chilly but not overcast.

We stood with her, our ears eager. What did it matter? Maybe she would see that we were sisters—we hadn't told her yet; or she would see that I had a husband and an eighteen-month-old son in Houston, which I also hadn't told her yet. A little prediction here, a little prophecy there. Like I said, a little fun to add some pep to the day. After all, this was my first getaway as a new mom. It was the end of summer 2002. I held out my right palm and she took it in the cusp of her hand, peering at it like a scientist into a microscope.

The smile on her face immediately vanished. Her face turned pale.

There was silence as she slowly looked up at me. Her eyes were narrowed. She studied my face and then looked back down into my palm. She looked up again at me.

"What's going on with you?" she asked. "Is anything stressful going on?"

"What do you mean?" I said.

"What's happening in your life?"

"I'm married," I replied.

"Mm hmm?"

"I have a toddler son, and I'm newly married. No big issues." My mouth was a little dry. Why was she asking me these questions? Was something wrong?

The psychic looked at her watch. "Can you meet me at the church at five p.m.? I want to pray with you." She pleaded with me more than once and pointed in the direction of the church.

I saw my sister Pauline's eyes fill with worry. She also had questions. Already, I could feel a nervous tingle in my back. My hands suddenly felt heavy, and I let them drop to my sides. This wasn't what I'd bargained for. It was meant to be a simple chit-chat and a gift of some thank-you money and off we would be to continue shopping and walking around.

The psychic turned to my sister, who presented her own palm. The lady lightened up as she studied Pauline's palm. Soon they were laughing and conversing between themselves while I stood staring. *What the hell?* I'd just been dealt a shitty reading and there they were, laughing away! My world had suddenly changed, a black cloud had fallen over me. My stomach had an upside-down feeling, as if I had been punched in the gut. They were acting like nothing had happened.

I called Raul, my husband, and broke into tears. He said to me, "Kristin, it's just a psychic. Don't take it seriously."

"But something will happen! I could see it in her eyes. She thinks something bad will happen!"

"Look it's okay. Is Pauline there with you?"

"Yes."

"You two go and have fun. You've never been the type to be afraid of a psychic's words."

I couldn't have fun; there was no way my mind could ignore this. Our shopping and fun ended abruptly. I told Pauline I could no longer remain on the streets. Our brother, Sy, picked us up on Stockton Street between Post and Geary. Inside his beaten-up silver Mazda, I was crying and in the darkest mood. I kept going on about the psychic, but tried to compose myself quickly, as Sy brushed me off as a dramatic sister.

I was shaken to bits. My insides were cold, and my blood was streaming heavily. The one thought that kept running through me was: *Why did the woman say that?* What had she seen etched into my palm? I was not superstitious and never had been. I did not come from a superstitious family, though I remember seeing my mother pour water after my father's car when he went on business trips. It was prayer for a safe return: Go like water, come back like water. Was that superstitious? I don't know. Hmmm, Mom and our Armenian family would carry around the evil eye for protection, good karma, and positive energies. We would also carry around the rosary or cross, could that be superstitious? No, I don't think so. I was overwhelmed, thinking how it didn't make sense to consider any of this superstitious behavior. I still believed that there were unexplainable things about life that could only be sensed with intuition. I guess I had inherited my mother's deep instincts. I could definitely sense something was very wrong.

The cloud in that psychic's eyes was a mix of worry and danger. It was like the look you would get in your eyes if a bad dream just came alive before you. What did she see that was too hard to say? I wished I could read her mind. My sister watched me from the other end of the hotel room, helpless to do anything.

I called my husband again. As I lay sobbing and talking to him, I debated on whether to meet the psychic at the church.

I didn't go.

Part One

Between a Rock and a Hard Place

The coldest winter I ever saw
was the summer I spent in San Francisco.

—Mark Twain

1

The Dive

The horn blew loudly in the early fog. All of us triathletes were standing on the edge of the boat, set for the dive. I said my prayers to give me the courage to plunge into the arctic waters, an ice-cold fifty degrees of the San Francisco Bay. Wet suit on and ready to swim, I wasn't going to be the first to make the dive, but I certainly would not be the last.

It was a chilly, cloudy morning that August day in 1999, and the sun was rising quickly. Earlier, the white ferry had arrived at the city-side dock where we all marched and boarded one by one. It felt sort of strange being in a race where I didn't know a single person. I felt lonely. As time progressed, I noticed no one knew anyone. Crammed into the lower deck of the ferry like sardines, we developed an automatic feeling of fellowship—we all picked the Alcatraz Challenge because it spoke to us.

There must have been at least three hundred triathletes; faces reached as far as the eyes could see. I knew the upper deck was similarly filled with people, possibly looking out into the waters as I was and considering their next move. As we approached the island, I became increasingly nervous about plunging into the frigid water.

The boat proceeded north and dropped its anchor adjacent to the island. It rocked back and forth in the choppy waters while I tried to prepare myself for the coming challenge.

This was the twenty-first Alcatraz Challenge, a triathlon comprising of a one-and-a-half-mile swim, a thirteen-mile bike ride, and a ten-mile run. I was ready at the young age of twenty-four; I had a lot of things to achieve. Before me was the famous Alcatraz penitentiary; behind me was the city of San Francisco. Before me was a triathlon I had never attempted before; behind me was a broken-off fairy-tale engagement. Before me were questions about what to do with this burning ambition for a successful and positive life; behind me was a Bachelor of Science degree from Stephen F. Austin State University.

One could hear a pin drop. My mind was racing. These shark-infested waters had been risky to escapee inmates with no wet suits and could be just as risky to us triathletes. Or were the sharks harmless? Maybe I was making up stories in my head.

Do I really want to do this? I asked myself. *I could die. I could die.*

The feeling was familiar. During a class presentation in sixth grade, I recall wishing the ground would open up and swallow me whole. In 1985, in Katy, Texas, I was the new kid in town from Dhahran, Saudi Arabia. I was so nervous as I read my work out loud to a class of querying eyes at Memorial Parkway Junior High. I thought I could die in front of all those eyes—most of all the eyes of Carl, my crush with shaggy blond hair. But I knew I had to do it, I just had to.

Now, by the famous Alcatraz prison—where Al Capone had been an inmate and from which Frank Lee Morris and the Anglin Brothers escaped back in 1962—an eerie feeling settled over my stomach. Their escape remains a mystery, as their bodies were never found. To think they had left one world for another, a prison for yet another prison—the idea gave me an awful sensation. To be a prisoner of anything would be a nightmare, to be confined in a little space forever. Little did I know that a certain type of prison was in my future.

I pulled out my yellow swim cap, put it over my head, and gathered my hair behind both ears. I will never forget the words on it: "Alcatraz Challenge: Between a Rock and a Hard Place." No kidding there. That had been my life this past year, to say the least. The script had described me in four words. I had come out of a broken engagement, ended another relationship, and was now about to dunk myself in a frozen sea of unknowns.

The second horn blew, signaling the start of the race. A grizzly, gray-bearded man announced it was time to make the jump. All around me, people were diving off the deck. I hesitated, then plunged in feet first. Not knowing the depth, I didn't want to go headfirst. The one-and-a-half-mile swim to the mainland had begun!

I took off with freestyle strokes. I remembered my swim team years in elementary school in the American compound in Dhahran, Saudi Arabia. During races at the Dhahran pool, Coach

Dennis, who had trained our "Neptunes" team would call out, "Pull, pull, Kristin!" I would pull my arms while swimming the freestyle, anxious to be the golden girl of our team. I made a conscious note to myself to do the breaststroke if I was out of breath.

Once I hit the water, I decided to implement my backup plan, as I felt better breathing fully with the breaststroke compared to limited breathing on one side while doing the freestyle. This was an old and useful trick. I kept going back to Coach Dennis's simple instructions, given in his South African accent.

The wet suit, which was sort of bulky, became fitted in the water. My visibility was diminished as I moved along. I could maybe see six inches in front of me. The murky waters wouldn't give much more. With every third stroke, I would take a breath for air and see the yellow of the safety canoes. They were in the front, middle, and back. They were all along the perimeter of the swimming crowd. My mind filled with the fear of sharks. There are nearly a dozen known species of sharks in the bay, both bottom dwelling and sand sharks, but as I later learned, most of them don't pay attention to humans.

I have the soul of a mermaid, I repeated to myself. At least that's what I've read about people born in December: soul of a mermaid, fire of a lioness, and heart of a hippie. Keep going—no quitting allowed. I had been training for months through the deep, hot summers of Houston, swimming about a hundred laps in my apartment pool most days, running approximately forty miles a week on the nature-trail loop at the city's Memorial Park, and using the elliptical machine and stationary bike at the gym to build mileage and endurance in the legs and cardiovascular system.

As a slender, young, exercise therapist, my metabolism was on high gear. I burned a lot of calories even though I ate everything and anything—chocolate chip cookies and Baskin Robbins chocolate ice cream being my favorite treats. Honestly, anything chocolate would go a long way. Unfortunately, I can no longer eat the same way now that I am in my forties.

When I left Houston the day before the triathlon, the sunflowers were in full bloom. My four-hour plane ride to San Francisco was safe, and my big brother, Sy, was waiting at the arrival terminal with hands in his pockets. He said, "What's up, Dawg?" It was his usual greeting for me since high school days because my friends would sometimes call me Dawg. It was also Sy's way of teasing me about my Texas accent. He jested about what I was wearing, and I remember we shared jokes about family. We loved to imitate Mom's accent. Mom was a dear and such an innocent angel. We were lucky to have her as our Mom, especially now, after learning of everyone's hardships with their mom or dad. Growing up, Sy and I were always close. Then with his high school years being spent in New Mexico, I rarely saw him, and we had grown apart. But our unspoken bond was always there.

He had set up my room with clean sheets, like I was a special guest. I slept like a baby. At four thirty the next morning, I jumped out of bed after hearing the alarm. I immediately turned it off and then walked hurriedly over to the bathroom, splashed my face with warm water, then changed into my race wear. *Today is my day*, I thought to myself. *I am really doing this!* I had on my favorite blue Speedo running shorts and a jog bra, which I had specifically purchased for race day. I popped a bagel, lots of water, and a purple Powerade for electrolytes. Off I was, out the door of Sy's apartment in the upper Haight-Ashbury district of San Francisco.

It was a charming neighborhood located just east of Golden Gate Park, which drew hippies. It reminded me of the old lyric "Be sure to wear some flowers in your hair" from a sixties song about San Francisco by Scott McKenzie. I've always found myself so drawn to this time and place. Perhaps it had to do with something about a past life. Who knows?

Getting a cab that morning was easy. At 5:00 a.m. the streets were peaceful and quite empty. After about ten minutes in the small taxi, I was dropped off at the pier. From the distance, I could see Alcatraz Island. Glancing at the choppy blue water, the Mark Twain quote came to mind: "The coldest winter I ever spent was a summer in San Francisco." Obviously, he was absolutely right with his thoughts, as there was icy air blowing on my skin even at the end of summer.

The fog was overbearing too.

Yes, I was. Yes, I was doing this.

Ten minutes into the race, I looked up and saw the island in front of me. The unmistakable greenery of the knolls, the tall lighthouse, and the jagged landscape sent a jolt of terror through me. It was like being in a machine in which the wheels were always sure to return you to the same spot no matter how hard you steered.

Holy shit, the current's got me! I thought.

Panicked, I made a curve, turning my body around to what I thought was the San Francisco shoreline. I had no idea I was swimming back toward Alcatraz Island. What was going on? The island was just there behind me, and here it was, still before me. I would not let swimming against the tide get me. I quickly made another turn. The bay area was before me again.

Agh, this can't happen again. I'm losing time.

I pulled myself even faster, making sure to keep up with more breaststrokes at this point. My arms worked furiously. My mind tried to maintain focus. All I had to worry about was the race. No, that was not all. My failed engagement came to my thoughts. I could see his face before me. He was handsome and brown-haired. A well-mannered Southern boy with ambition and focus. He'd always been sincere about his feelings for me. But for some reason or another, our fantasy love began to crumble.

The night we broke the engagement, our sense of truth to one another had spoken. I gave him back the ring, like a solid transaction, peeling it off my finger and leaving that space blank. I'm positive that if we were more mature, we could, as adults, talk over our differences. Obviously, our minds were too young. I called everybody, and bad news travels fast. I don't even remember if email was around then. Wedding invitations had already been sent out a week prior, so my Mom called people to say there was a new development. Mom's dear friend Bunny also informed guests of the disengagement.

Some months later, I met Ted, a girlfriend's brother, who used to be in the Marine Corps. He had an athletic build, ice-blue eyes, and fair skin. He seemed nice, I would say, until he gave me a Bible, with my first name and last initial, "S," inscribed on the cover.

Did he just give me a Bible? I thought.

I'm the first one to love the Bible. But having my last name inscribed on it was way too much too soon to handle. His last name was Smith, mine was Saleri. Why was he silently inferring we had a future together by emphasizing the "S"? This was another sign of too much too soon. Or was I overthinking it? Regardless, I didn't want this type of complexity after my disengagement. I was trying to live like a free spirit with no intense relationships, no commitments.

Agh, to hell with all of this. I decided I wasn't going to let anybody douse my positive spirit. This Alcatraz Challenge, as my first official race, was a way for me to do something new for myself and wash away the bad taste of these relationships. Starting fresh is all I wanted.

I now had my eyes on the shore as I swam harder than ever. I glanced at my black Timex watch. It was about forty minutes into the swim event of the triathlon. I couldn't believe I was keeping up with a fast-paced swim group. I was exceeding my expectations for myself at this point.

"Pull, Kristin!" Coach Dennis's voice kept echoing.

My head was in line with my body; my shoulders, hips, and legs tugged at the core of my body. My neck strained as I kicked. This was a race for the bright daylight of the shoreline. I pulled with all of my strength. One, two, three. The shoreline approached. Or was I the one approaching it? The shoreline and I were becoming one. Swooshing my bare feet, which were completely numb at this moment, I was becoming one with the earth.

I saw the change station ahead. As I waded through the shallow waters, I checked my watch, then looked around and saw fit and competitive racers around me. How in the world did I keep up with them? If Coach Dennis could see me now.

As the Armenian saying goes: "Asdvadz hedit"—God is with you.

I climbed onto the concrete steps to change for the bike ride. I noticed that not only were my feet numb but my entire body was numb. My feet felt like iced bricks. How in the world was I going to run to the bike section of the race if I couldn't even feel my feet? I unzipped the wet suit while keeping my blue Speedo jog bra and bottoms on. I made sure to chug water from the orange and white jug they had at the changing station. I knew my purple Powerade would be waiting for me at the bike station. I laced up my Asics running shoes and pinned on my number 408 racing bib. *Good number*, I thought to myself. Even numbers are good, and ones that end in eight are especially lucky.

I was off on a mile-long warm-up run to the bike station. My extremities were anesthetized from the frozen waters. I was moving with no feet and was running on ice stubs. Was this normal? The feeling was similar to how I felt after my failed relationships. With me being me, I was trying to be positive; to look forward and do healthy things for myself. To get my blood flowing again, I had to stop worrying. It would come back; the feeling would come back, I knew it, I just had to keep moving. At the bike station, I downed a GU energy gel packet and a Powerade for a recharge. My limbs began waking up or warming up.

Biking was next.

This was my weak point, and I knew it. It was so hard to train in Houston traffic, and I would make do on the stationary bike, but it never gave me the challenge of live terrain. I had assumed I would fall behind on this thirteen-mile bike portion, so I was thankful I was able to gain a head start with the swim.

After clipping into my bike pedals, I knew this leg of the event would be strenuous. I could feel the lactic acid build up in my lower body. The weight of my legs was overbearing. Although I topped speeds of 22 mph on the bike, the hills were a killer. I would sometimes have to get off the bike and walk up the hills. The Houston hills were nothing like the hills in San Francisco. Really, there were no hills in Houston. My hands kept slipping off the handlebars from sweat. To calm myself, I reasoned that all I had to do was finish and not be competitive.

Although my instinct was to be competitive—it was my nature.

I knew I wanted to finish. I had to finish.

I was in the middle of the biking pack at this point. Mind over matter.

The trees zoomed past me like a silent audience, and the earth beneath my bike tires seemed to squeak an annoying message of hope. Instead of Coach Dennis's "Puuull!" I could hear the wind swishing by my face, my heartbeat pounding underneath the 408 bib. Go, go, go. I prayed. My feet pedaled on. Sometimes I got off and felt a little disappointed walking by my bike. After major focus and prayers, I'd jump back on and continue pedaling uphill. Dang, this was way harder than I thought. I'm sure other curse words were coming to mind.

At the finish of the bike portion of the race, I excitedly jumped off as though at a party with friends. The hard part was over; it was time for the run, my favorite part. Thank God. I kept wiping sweat from my forehead in the seventy-degree sun. I loved the warm sun. It made the run through the redwoods visually awesome and beautiful, to say the least. As my feet sank in the sand while I ran on the beachfront, I thought of the freedom the best running Kenyans must experience doing this by hillsides and free landscapes. There was a freedom to be had in nature. It was a recipe for being in the best shape ever, body, mind, and spirit.

The stepladder approached, and although I dreaded the four hundred Sand Ladder steps that incline along the side of the cliff, I told myself to focus a little at a time instead of looking straight up to see how far I had to go. This section was a killer. I had hit a wall. How did racers survive this part? Every time I thought I was done there were ten more steps to go!

Entering the final stretch of the ten-mile run, I felt the excitement rush through my body. I was about to have this race under my belt. The completion of this triathlon would be a rebirth for me, the start of a new beginning. A clean slate.

As I ran that last hundred yards on the hot black pavement with the bay to the left of me, my brother and Rachael, my old college friend and roommate, were cheering me on! I was doing the "Saleri Sprint" as my husband would come to call it a few years later. I could feel the heat seeping through my Asics running shoes. My palms were clammy with the sweat of excitement.

I crossed the finish line with the big timer above reading my time in red: "Ultimate Escape, 3:41:13." There were cheering crowds and a big white banner above.

Finally, I had the Alcatraz Challenge under my belt!

That evening as I celebrated with Sy and his friends at an American-cuisine restaurant, there were big cheers and laughter around our table. It was perhaps the first group laughter I had enjoyed since the broken engagement. There was something indescribably special about this moment because the phases of the run had somehow stripped layers off me. The swim had baptized me, and I felt newly refreshed and exhilarated. The bike and run had given me a new appreciation for my body. The final run itself was a push for completion—a statement of my potency and inner grit to succeed as a woman newly graduated from a small college in Nacogdoches, the oldest town in Texas.

Back at home, in Houston, I spread the news. I had survived the sharks, and the elements of the water. My coworkers knew I'd completed the challenge, and they were all very congratulatory and complimenting, saying things like "You are at your fighting weight." We would all laugh, and I would say my thank-yous. That Alcatraz race was the first of many planned races that would lead to my inner desire to be an elite athlete, with the Ironman as my ultimate finish line.

I had found what was to be my real path in life, or so I thought. I had dreams to remain single until thirty, and then have three kids by age thirty-three. We all have dreams and goals, right? Plans. I had it mapped out in my mind. I knew I didn't fit the mold of a traditional college-marriage-children storyline, or what the American-Armenian standards said. It was clear to me at this time that I would explore a career in physical therapy or dietetics, and in the custom of the young fire within me, I had to charge forward.

Puuull, Kristin!

2

What the Hell was That?

The hand of God was at work when I first sighted Raul, the man who would become my husband. It was a casual sighting, a near accident. It was a few months after the Alcatraz Challenge, on a September evening. I had recently moved to the Creole Apartments off San Felipe, and not far away was the Q Club, a gym I began to patronize almost religiously when I wasn't running at Memorial Park. One day, as I pulled into the parking lot of the Q Club in my white Maxima, I almost hit a young man who seemingly popped out of nowhere.

"Oh shoot," I said, slamming on the breaks. I waved as I slowly drove by. Cute guy.

He looked to be in a hurry as he walked toward his green Ford Bronco, carrying his workout bag.

Raul walked into my life again, months later, when my childhood friend Keely set us up on a blind date. I remember driving along Allen Parkway when she called me in excitement.

"Kristin," she said, "there's this guy who I think you should meet."

"Well, what's his name?" I asked. "Raul."

"Keely," I said. "Are you sure? Is he my type?"

"Oh, come on," she said. "He's a really good dancer and so cute."

Online dating had just become popular—there was no swiping to the left or right quite yet. Things were still old-school, and my friends were always there to back me up in finding someone, as I was open to the dating scene.

We were meeting at the popular Little Pappasito's Cantina, before the Houston Rockets game, and I ended up arriving about forty minutes late because I was debating whether to go in or not. For support, I called my brother Sy in San Francisco. Thankfully he answered and I proceeded to ask him his thoughts on the scenario. If I should go ahead and meet him.

"When is the date, Kristin?" asked Sy.

Pausing for a second, with a slight shakiness in my voice and biting my lips,

"Right now," I replied.

I knew, as I said this, I had to get out of the car, walk in, and meet my blind date.

"Well then go in!" said Sy. "How backwards and rude, Kristin." At that point, we ended up hanging up the phone. But, needing more support, I quickly dialed my friend Heather's number on my silver Nokia phone. What were her honest thoughts? I just knew she would tell me the truth. As I sat in the parking lot, our dialogue went on discussing how I had just gotten out of two relationships and was not yet ready for a new one. I wasn't ready for any new male in my life. I remember thinking, as the light bulb went off in my mind, *there is nothing wrong with meeting new people*. From that thought, and from something uplifting Heather or Sy must have said, I made up my mind to go in.

As I walked confidently into Little Pappasito's, I saw Keely, Kale and Raul staring at me. Seeing Raul, I thought, *Wait, I've seen this face somewhere.*

He stood up at the table and shook my hand. "Hi, I'm Raul."

He was a gentleman in jeans, a collared shirt, and boots. A typical Texas A&M Aggie— clean cut, young, and handsome. He had an attractive, intriguing look about him that went perfectly with his eyes, which were dancing with happiness, and his dark hair. There was something about him. His big brown eyes were the best part of him, and today I still say they're like Hershey Kisses. We immediately clicked. Mexican food, Coronas, and great conversation were being passed around the table. Throughout dinner as we all talked, he would cross his arms on the table and speak in his serious but quiet voice. Something about him made me smile internally.

We laughed and compared stories, as we were fairly new college graduates from A&M, Stephen F. Austin, and Southwest. Later, that evening, we attended the Rockets game where we noticed we also shared a similar sense of humor. We had spotted a lady walking down the ramp, and Raul and I suddenly turned to each other and laughed at her neon green tube top mismatched with her shorts and red stilettos. We were young and rude.

At the end of our evening of fun he said to me, "I need an out. I have a family wedding coming up next week and need a friend to accompany me. Will you come with me?"

I accepted. It was our first formal date.

Everything happens for a reason, and I was in love not long after. I was secretly worried, though, because when Raul finally proposed, I'd barely known him for a year. But I reminded myself that my parents had only known each other for two weeks before they got engaged. This was an affirmation to me that time did not matter.

We had our baby boy in December of 2000. Raul and I named him Jacob after my grandfather—Hagop in Armenian and Jacob in English. To this day, my side of the family calls my son Hagop, and his father's Cuban side of the family calls him Jacobo, which is Spanish for Jacob. As I was dilating to give birth to my first-born son, my body decided to act differently. My dilation went backward instead of forward. Who knew this could even happen? As my temperature escalated to 101°F, Jacob was also "burning up," as the nurse exclaimed at the time.

Born after an eighteen-hour-long labor and emergency C-Section, Jacob was welcomed to the world as a big baby, at eight pounds and eleven ounces. Unfortunately, due to both the surgery and my fever, I could not hold my first born until the next day, after both of our fevers subsided. I hated that. I knew we both were lacking the crucial bonding time of mother and baby.

Doctors and nurses had to follow protocol—Jacob was immediately whipped away from me the instant after he was born.

Later, I was wheeled to him in NICU and only able to touch him from a distance. He was laying in his open bed warmer. I so wanted to be able to hold him but knew I would have to wait. Both of us were not in good shape at that moment.

God, I couldn't wait to hold him.

The next morning, I was holding Jacob—was this real? I felt like I had been visited by an angel, was I really holding my baby?

Were Raul and I really parents?

After Jacob's birth, I was back to my prebirth weight in two weeks. Now I know that that was a gift because with my second child, Colin, my former body never returned. I'm still fighting post-pregnancy weight gain, long after sixteen years.

The arrival of Jacob was a transitional time, a hardship for the both of us as young parents and newlyweds. A rollercoaster of ups, downs, and all arounds. We went from being free young people one day to being married and parents the next. We were twenty-six years old, not necessarily a young age, but young enough that we had not experienced the dating scene like we should have. In all reality, we faced challenges that made us wonder if we knew each other as well as we thought we did. Raul was frequently going out for golf outings with friends while I stayed home and played new mother to Jacob.

Suddenly, I had gone from enjoying a very active social scene to experiencing a stricter regime of abrupt motherhood.

Our first year was a whirlwind. Raul and I had a tough time acclimating to our new normal. We both made mistakes as young newlyweds with a newborn and first child. Who doesn't? You

live and learn, right? I recall a time when baby Jacob was crying
heavily in the middle of the night like most infants do. This was
a colicky cry, a restless cry. Jacob was right down the hall from us
on the second story of our tiny townhome in midtown Houston.

I walked over and held him and tried my hardest to make
him stop crying.

I nudged Raul who would pry one eye open.

"I need your help. Can you try? The poor guy will not stop
crying."

Raul cradled Jacob and did the same thing as I did. Then he
would come back to wake me. "Your turn."

This went on for hours.

I then remembered a trick I'd read about ways to calm babies.
It mentioned placing restless babies on a dryer set to tumble dry
low. The sensations and sounds of the soft whirls would help
the baby relax. If that didn't work, I was going on to the next
trick picked from my newborn books. This one said to turn on
the faucet and place the baby close by. The sounds of running
water would soothe the baby in five to ten minutes. I first tried
the dryer method and sure enough, it worked. My baby dozed
off restfully. I returned him to the crib and laid him on his
tummy. His ankles would cross over one another. Too cute. I sat
and gazed at his cuteness a while. Nothing quite as peaceful as
watching your very own sleep.

As I lay on the full-size bed next to his yellow Stephanie Anne
crib, I could hear gunshots and people yelling outside. They were
either homeless or coming out from the halfway house down the

street. The bed leaned against the bay windows, and one could hear and see anything on the streets. When Jacob was breastfeeding, frantic yelling from drug dealers could be heard all over the neighborhood. It was certainly not a calm middle-of-the-night scene. I knew this was not the place to bring up our newborn.

During the day, Mimi, Jacob's babysitter, would look after him while I went to work. She was good at entertaining him with songs like "Donde ta la Luna," at which point Jacob would stare wide-eyed at her fingers pointed in the air and waving from side to side. Mimi's song was about the stars and moon and her fingers mimicked their motions in the sky.

At night Raul and I would be back to our routine. He cared for Jacob while I slept and vice versa. We would tag team. By morning I'd be off again to Texas Children's Hospital where I worked as an exercise therapist for children. One day, as I was washing dishes and inadvertently slamming them into the dishwasher, I looked up and saw Raul looked the same as me. Our eyes were tired and mine were especially puffy. New parenthood, the drug dealing ruckus, and lack of sleep was catching up to us.

"This is too much," I said. I brought it up to him that we needed to move. He immediately agreed. It only made sense for his parents and sister's family to live nearby and help us. We sure needed all the help we could get. Everything was changing and changing fast. I guess I have to get use to this, I would say, crying to myself. It was actually the ugly cry that would happen in private. Living in the city with an infant was not a perfect scenario especially with the background drug dealers. We had to make that change sooner than later. Gosh, everyone on my side of the family were living their own happy lives in their respective cities. On the other hand, I was somewhat lonely and wished my family was in the area to help support my new family life. With my parents in Saudi Arabia, brother in San Francisco, and my sister in Chicago, I knew this would not happen. I had to put my big girl pants on and there was no time for sappy cries and getting emotional. I was a new wife and mother who wanted to be good at it. This is all the new normal and I have to make it good, and it will be good. That was that.

Months later, we moved to Canyon Gate in Richmond, a suburb outside Houston.

Sleepless, chaotic nights soon gave way to arguments and fights. I was still working at the Texas Children's Hospital, but things were getting complicated because of the new marriage and new motherhood. Although Mimi was great with Jacob, I developed some sort of maternal panic that my son would not see me as his full mother. I wanted and needed to spend more time with my son.

"You don't have to work," Raul said. "You can always stay home."

"Yes, I do have to work," I disagreed. "I love working with kids. This is what I went to school for. It's my job and I love what I do."

Raul was annoyed. I had to make up my mind and heart on what I really wanted. At the end, I resigned my job to spend more time with the baby.

My parents would visit from Saudi Arabia, where Dad worked, two or three times a year. My mother was a successful preschool teacher in Dhahran. She ran a school out of a renovated garage. This was usually the thing for young mothers in Saudi Arabia to do. There were many preschools around, but Mom's "Wonderful Little People" was always known to be the best.

Dad held an influential position with Saudi Aramco, the national oil company of Saudi Arabia and the world's largest oil company. As head of reservoir management, he was responsible for managing its entire oil production, as well as the stewardship of its reserves that accounted for roughly 25 percent of the global total. Whenever Dad came into Houston for meetings, they always stayed in our home in Richmond's newly developed subdivision of Canyon Gate.

They visited one day in 2002 when the fall weather was close to eighty degrees, with a full yellow sun and a warm blue sky. It was typical Houston weather. By this time of year in September it had begun cooling to the eighties during the day and upper sixties in the nights. It was around five on a Saturday evening when we started craving Italian food. We picked Perry's Italian, a restaurant in the New Territory area. It was ten minutes away. We piled into our Toyota Sequoia and the five of us were off to dinner.

The street was quiet as we drove along. The neighborhood of Canyon Gate was vastly different from the noisy one in midtown. Although Raul and I didn't know anybody, people were always friendly and ready to engage socially. Our neighborhood would always have social events for parents from dinner parties to bunko groups or anything in between. Something was always taking place and quite often. Actually, it would turn out that a wine dinner was being held at around the same time a couple blocks away.

With Jacob aged one and a half, we had to make sure to be done with dinner by 5:30 or 6:00 p.m. at the latest. Not doing this meant it would be a tough evening getting our "big guy" to sleep due to an uncomfortable colic he had dealt with since infancy. Regardless of the Mylicon and soy milk our wonderful pediatrician, Dr. Boardman, recommended, Jacob always cried and whined too much, more so in the evenings. Poor little guy. "Colic," Dr. Boardman always said. "It's colic." Even with the other antacids he would prescribe, we were still at a dead-end with this.

The medicine may have worked—sometimes. Personally, I thought it rarely worked. Too bad there was no user manual for new parents or for new parents with a colicky baby. I am positive that, in these days of social media, this information is available all over.

At times, Raul would have to take Jacob out for hours in a countryside car ride at night. He would always have his wintergreen dip in his back pocket or perfectly situated on the side door of his truck. Upon entering his truck, a small pinch of his wintergreen on his bottom lip would do the trick. It helped make the night drive more tranquil for crying baby and stressed out Raul. Baby J would almost always fall asleep in his car seat. My son was hurting, and only if we had the right "calm my belly down" medicine would it be easier for him to go to sleep.

I thought it would be easier tonight though, since my parents were here to give some support, and truth be told, my Mom had a way with my little son that I was still trying to catch up with. Such a cute, chubby, and handsome baby Jacob was. He was mostly bald his first year of life and now his brown hair had grown in. The funny thing was that his favorite show to watch at the time was Caillou, a cartoon series of a bald young boy. In his toddler years, Jacob's brown hair was so pretty, with light-brown coloring and natural highlights to compliment it. Still today, he has a beautiful head of hair worth envying.

Sitting in a booth with the quiet dark ambiance of the casual Italian eatery, we ordered our usual: plain spaghetti with butter for Jacob, chicken parmesan for Raul, spaghetti with marinara for me, grilled eggplant for Mom, and a spaghetti with meatballs for Dad. And of course, a meal without a Caesar salad is not a meal, and Dad ordered that too.

We continued talking.

"I have my last long training run tomorrow," I said to the table as I enjoyed my spaghetti. I had run my first marathon in Chicago the year before and was now getting ready for my second in Washington, DC. This year I was running for a reason: the St. Jude's Children's Hospital. My Dad's twin brother Alen, a doctor who lived in Potomac, had convinced me to participate. I was helping to raise money for the children of St. Jude's while doing something I loved—running. I was excited to be a part of it all. It didn't get better than this—giving to young children in need.

"I'll go with you for half the run," Raul said encouragingly. "I can bring you Powerade and water."

"Oh, perfect. Thank you!"

I was relieved, as it meant I could run in our subdivision and wouldn't have to get up extra early, at 5:00 a.m., and drive into town to meet my running group. Being away from busy city life and living in the outer suburbs of Houston was nice and calming. Raul being by my side would make things easier.

My parents agreed to take care of Jacob in the morning. Everything was working out perfectly. Parenthood is easier when you have a team behind you. Actually, anything is, with the right kind of support. We were thrilled my parents were present not only because they are my parents but because Raul could run with me that next morning.

As we finished our dinner, Jacob became more restless and that was our sign he was ready to go. Before coffee was offered by our waitress, Dad asked for the check. We caravanned home and Jacob immediately fell asleep, like a quiet and peaceful little angel. I wondered if it was because my parents were with us.

My parents stayed up awhile drinking chamomile tea.

Raul and I retired to bed, looking forward to the morning.

Sunrise is faithful. It is universal. It happens every twenty-four hours. The peaceful sound of the morning is inviting, tranquil, and devoid of strain. As I awoke on Sunday, September 29, 2002, at 6:30 a.m., my body felt relaxed with quiet awareness. It was Raul's Mom's birthday. We would call her after our long run, although she was probably awake at the time.

Houston that morning was bright with clear blue skies. The overpowering beauty was inviting all of the city to enjoy the outdoors. Raul and I had not run together very often since the birth of Jacob, unless there was someone to watch him at home. This morning, as we were leaving, Dad played with Jacob in the living room as Mom slept.

We popped a bite of a plain bagel and had a shot of bittersweet Starbucks coffee. Raul and I laced up our running shoes and did some quick stretches in the garage. He usually liked to stretch longer than me. I knew it was good for my body, but I always wanted to get the run started.

An extra feeling of ease rushed through me knowing that he would be with me on my last long training run, before my big marathon day. We had been running together for two years. Although he was a much faster runner, I liked to brag that I could practice, practice, and practice some more; but he was always better than me. I would find out later that he wasn't as in love with running as I was and did it mostly for my sake. After twenty years together, I acknowledge that running is not his first exercise of choice!

This morning I felt confident. I had prepared religiously for the Marine Corp Marathon in the past six months. Now it was only four short weeks away, and I couldn't be any more satisfied with my progress. The year prior, at the Chicago Marathon, I had done okay for my standards: four hours and thirty minutes. For my second marathon, I knew I would have an improved finish time because I was running to give life to children in need.

Out the garage and off we went by 7:00 a.m. It was so quiet outside.

Raul and I looked at one another. "Let's get this started!"

We loved each other so, and this next year and a half was sure to be proof of that.

"Thanks for running the first part with me, babe," I said. "I truly appreciate it."

Since it was a long eighteen-mile run, I made sure to start slow. The air was crisp, not too hot yet, as fall was in the air. You could see and smell the fresh pink petunias in bloom. It was a clean and refreshing smell, even for suburban Houston. No cars were on the street this Sunday morning.

I wore my blue jogging top, running shorts, Asics running shoes, and a Polo Ralph Lauren cap with an imprint of the American flag. I had worn that very ball cap since college days. From Greek Week to relaxed days, my hat was always on as I went from happy hours in the pool and patios with college friends to fitness runs, after college days. Fitted backward, it was always snug on my face—my go-to look.

We jogged outside of our cul-de-sac on Weirgate Lane in the Canyon Gate subdivision, onto the main road, keeping it slow as it was the beginning of our run. We passed the basketball courts and the workout center. I would sometimes use this workout center when Raul would get home from work and watch Jacob.

"Let's go out nine miles and run through Greatwood," I said, "then loop back in. We should run faster, but this pace will be good enough for today." After all, we were both twenty-seven and very capable of running as fast as we pleased.

Canyon Gate was nestled in the woods down Crabb River Road, across from Greatwood. The neighborhood usually had low traffic, and Raul and I ran shoulder to shoulder on the sidewalk. Sometimes Raul would go in front, and I would follow.

At this point, I was still waking up, not being much of a morning person. I hoped we would be done by 10:00 a.m. in order to enjoy the full day with my parents and Jacob. I thought of the delicious morning breakfast that awaited me. I craved a big breakfast, with large pancakes, crispy bacon, and over-easy eggs. My favorites were the ones from Buffalo Grill—spreading the soft, cubed butter on the pancakes, with just a little drizzle of hot syrup, would make the most delicious pancakes. That was their signature, the hot syrup. It still is eighteen years later.

Raul was in front of me with his long running strides. About five foot eight and a fast runner, he always moved like it was easy and required no effort. With his natural athletic build and broad shoulders, I told myself it must be a genetic thing. I had to work at my speed; for him, it was natural. Annoying to me, since I had to work hard at what I got but lucky for him, ha!

I found a moment during my run to fix my cap. At the same time, I rearranged my sunglasses to shield me from the growing intensity of the sun's glare. I thought how glad I was to wear my new Asics running shoes and break them in one month before race day, at the end of October. I rechecked my pockets for my chocolate GU. I religiously brought adequate amounts on training runs—they would keep the energy balance going. I felt three in my back short pocket, plenty to get me through the next couple of hours.

That morning, I remember feeling thankful and positive. It was a beautiful day, with the overpowering beauty of the distant sun still rising on the horizon and beaming. It glowed. When I signed up for the Marine Corps Marathon, we were offered the option of designating our race to a charity. As I was naturally pulled toward helping others and children, the St. Jude's Hospital option caught my interest.

Thoughts of the kids I worked with at Texas Children's blended with the pounding of my Asics on the sidewalk. One of my favorite patients was battling Prader Willi syndrome and the other, Down syndrome. I had once taken them to Six Flags AstroWorld for the day, and there was not a roller coaster that we missed. The Texas Cyclone was their favorite. Marilyn and John had hopped on the wooden roller coaster once the gates pushed open. As the buckles clicked over their shoulders, I could hear their giggling from where I sat behind them.

Starting out slow, and creeping uphill, the roller coaster ascended steadily. It would pause for about five seconds, giving the kids time for the anticipation to build up, and then plunge downward, going about 75 mph. John and Marilyn would throw their arms in the air, laughing aloud and staring at each other. They gasped and screamed. All three of us held on for our lives. As we got off the roller coaster, their hollering laughter was priceless. I gave them water to hydrate, and we later stopped to eat a healthy snack.

"Let's do it again," they told me.

"One time is enough guys," I said. "And there are plenty more rides."

Next thing you know, we'd ended up doing it again, and then we ventured on our way to find many more rides in the park. It was our lucky day, no lines during the week. With Prader Willi, John had the challenge of never feeling satiety when he ate. Prader Willi patients usually possess an overweight body type. John also struggled with behavioral problems, intellectual disability, and an atypical short stature due to hormonal complications. I came in to help with his obesity as an exercise therapist as much as with Marilyn, whose Down syndrome had led to developmental delays. Both of my patients Marilyn and John were angels on Earth.

Finally, I had to be the bearer of bad news and tell them it was time to wrap it up. They couldn't have enough of the Texas Cyclone. "It's time go home," I said. "We've had a long and fun day at the park."

Back to the training run, passing the Canyon Gate guard shack, my husband and I turned right on Sansbury, where the sidewalk ended. At this point we detoured to the left simultaneously.

We made our way to the median, continuing our slow warm-up pace.

Oh good, I thought to myself, *the mile marker is right up there, at Crabb River Road*. This was the spot where we would always stop for a break and also to wait for cars to pass. My breathing was heavier now. I felt the pressure of an earlier paper cut on my right index finger as I wiped sweat off my forehead.

A car was approaching. It was a four-door Lumina sedan coming toward the guard shack, right where the sidewalk ends. The driver made his way through the exit of our Canyon Gate subdivision and, turning right on Sansbury Boulevard, headed north.

It drove up behind us.

Then it struck.

Suddenly, Raul felt a strong, cool wind swoosh by. It was a brush on his right shoulder.

"What the hell was that?" he shouted.

I had vanished from his side.

3

Gravity

In a blink of an eye, I was airlifted thirty-forty yards.

A catapult.

I abruptly landed on the hood of the sedan, smashing the driver's windshield. A bullet had struck the windshield. The bullet was a human—me. I slowly rolled off and splattered helplessly on my right side. I was making weird noises as blood gushed from my mouth and nose.

Raul rushed to me, yelling frantically.

I had just been dealt a death blow.

The driver maxed out at 25 mph on Sansbury Boulevard when he reached us. I later had cause to doubt that it was 25 mph. It must have been faster.

The driver, an off-duty policeman, got out of his car to see what he had hit, but Raul was yelling so much at the man that he stood aside. The driver was in shock, I would think, as he had just hit a human head on. He called 911. His statement says that at first, he wondered if he had hit a deer. "What was a deer doing out on 99?" he reasoned. According to him, we were close to the country but not in the country.

The evening before he had attended a get-together with friends in the neighborhood. That morning he was off to an early security shift at a church in Memorial as a second job. We had been strangers in the night and only blocks away from one another before this moment.

The sun was extremely bright on that morning of Sunday, September 29. It was so bright a flip-down visor could not block the overpowering sunlight. The sun blinded the driver as it rose over Sansbury Boulevard.

I lay in a puddle of blood. I was not responding, even though Raul kept talking to me.

"It's gonna be all right," he whispered.

I was unconscious and my legs were twitching uncontrollably.

A Canyon Gate neighbor who was enjoying some morning coffee on the porch with her husband heard the noise and ran over to her fence. She shouted to her husband to throw her a blanket. The Good Samaritan quickly jumped her backyard fence, handing Raul the blanket, which he put over me. Later we learned her name was Wafaa and she had taught at Raul's elementary school.

The sun was still coming up, beaming brightly.

I was breathing.

People were now pouring out of their houses.

The first medic that showed up wasn't in an ambulance; he was a fire department volunteer in a station wagon. He didn't know what to do until a real ambulance and the police showed up.

I was breathing, but heavily, like a snore. It was an uneasy sound.

Raul later told me everything was happening in a blur, and he'd never felt so afraid.

An Asian lady drove onto Sansbury Boulevard. I don't know her name to this day. But she gave Raul a silver angel medallion, saying, "She will be okay."

Another neighbor, a Middle Eastern lady, got our address from Raul and went to get my father.

Back home, Dad was drinking coffee or tea while reading his usual morning paper in a comfortable position on the floor. Jacob was playing not far away with his stick Gymboree, walking intently with the stick held upright on its colorful end. He had just been fed warm milk in his sippy cup, along with his favorite oatmeal and banana-puree cereal. He would make happy noises to Dad, who took the time to talk back to his first grandson. Mom was still in bed.

Dad heard a knock at the door. Thinking Raul and I were back from our run, he answered. It was the Good Samaritan.

"Does Kristin live here?" the woman asked.

Dad said, "Yes. Kristin lives in this house. Why're you asking?"

The woman said, "Everything is fine. She is fine, but Raul says that you have to come with me."

Immediately, Dad got the idea that something awful had happened, that I may not be alive. He went to Mom, who was just waking up. He leaned over, calling her "Ma." Dad always called Mom "Ma," short for Marina.

He whispered, "Ma, everything is okay. Everything is okay. Kristin had an accident and it's okay. It's okay. I have to go. You need to watch Jacob."

Dad would say, categorically, that it was the toughest moment of his life. He had to go over to wake Mom up, then watch her face as he told her something dreadful had happened, even though he didn't know all the details just yet. He was sure to stay very calm.

"She's been involved in an accident," was all he said.

Mom held her chest with both hands. Wearing only a nightgown, she became so cold that she had to put on her robe. Mom lost it internally, but she couldn't lose it externally too. She had Jacob and needed to be proactive and collected for him.

Inside, she began to say a prayer.

That was how my parents found out about the accident.

As Dad left, Mom called Raul's mother, Maky. She dialed once and hung up, unable to break the news.

She stood shaking, saying to herself, "Marina, you have to do this."

So, she dialed again. But the line was busy.

4

Life Flight

The neighbor took Dad to the scene five minutes away. He saw a crowd. He saw the fire engines, ambulances, and a lot of police monitoring the cordoned-off scene. There was an overhead helicopter. Instinctively, Dad barged through the crowd, because from a distance, from fifty yards away, he saw me lying on the road in a pool of blood. He wasn't sure whether I was dead or alive. He leaped over the police lines, and two cops stopped him. Dad later said that I was gone, or more definitively, dead. The only proof of life were my shaking legs.

"That's my daughter!" he yelled. "I need to know what's going on!"

As the helicopter was whirling in the background, the medics gave me injections to lower my body temperature as prevention of further damage at a cellular level. I later learned it was the induced coma regimen, a part of individual trauma management. I was being airlifted now, and the medics told Raul to meet the helicopter at Memorial Hermann. He naturally wanted to stay by my side. They couldn't let him go with me because family was not allowed on the flight.

On the Life Flight, the twenty-two-mile route to the hospital began. The nurses on board quickly inserted an airway suction cup and an endotracheal tube for intubation, to improve oxygen flow. This would then be connected to a mechanical ventilator at the hospital to help with breathing. Trauma protocol was being followed precisely, minute to minute, by the in-flight medics.

"If you can't see, you should stop driving!" Raul charged at the driver. "Did you deliberately hit my wife? How could you do this?"

"Sir, I would never do anything like that," he said. Those were the first and last words he ever said to my husband.

Dad had to restrain Raul and pull him away. They drove to the hospital for what Raul thought of as the most dreadful car ride of his life. Dad, who normally drives slowly, made Raul very upset because Dad obeyed stop signs and wasn't going at top speed. It was slower than a turtle's pace. That was the engineer in Dad. Under such stressful circumstances, he wanted to make sure that they didn't cause extra problems, to stay calm in this dire situation.

"Why are you going so slow?" Raul asked him. His wife was in danger! "Nansen, please, go faster," pleaded Raul.

I could imagine that Dad was going slow as molasses.

"Safety protocol, Raul," Dad replied. "We have to keep calm, as accidents usually take place when one has already taken place. I'm going as fast as we should."

As Dad and Raul were on their way, the doorbell rang back home.

Mom answered.

Another Good Samaritan delivered my Asics running shoes from the accident scene, as they had been left on the road.

The news spread. Maky, my mother-in-law—who was very much wrapped up in the spirit of her birthday celebration— heard the phone ring as she walked out the door for church at St. Laurence's, where Father Drew was the parish priest. She was with the rest of the family: Carlos, her husband, whom we call Buelo; Maky's mother, Martha, whom we called Abita; Raul's older sister (also named Martha); her husband, Dan, and their children.

On the phone's second ring, Maky turned back to answer the call, expecting it might be Raul calling to wish her a happy birthday. It was a family tradition to have her three kids call first thing in the morning to give celebratory birthday wishes.

She was right. It was Raul, but with frightening news. "Mom, there's been a bad accident," he said while choking up. "Kristin has been hit by a car."

As Raul was on the phone, one of the onsite medics in the background said, "She's in really, really bad shape, and she's probably not going to make it."

Immediately, Maky's birthday was forgotten.

Accidents come without invitation.

In a blink, our family changed plans. My sister-in-law, Martha, went to pick up Jacob and, thereafter, leave him in the hands of the family housekeeper, who was also looking after Martha's kids. Dan drove to pick up Mom to go the hospital in his "yellow banana" as we all called his vintage Mercedes Benz vehicle.

Everyone else piled into various cars, and Maky kept talking to Raul on the phone as they were on their way.

It was a caravan of cars.

Dad called Sy in San Francisco on the way there.

Along with Raul's brother, Carlos, the Abello and Saleri families arrived simultaneously, pouring into Memorial Hermann hospital like an army of dedicated defenders.

Brother arrived on day three.

Part Two

Aftershocks

If you are a dreamer, come in. For we have
some flax-golden tales to spin …

—Shel Silverstein

5

Seven Days

Raul and I are first-generation Americans. Our parents are immigrants—Raul's are from Cuba, and mine are Armenians from Istanbul. My parents had moved to the United States in 1970, many decades after the painful history of the 1915 Armenian genocide in which an estimated 1.5 million Armenians—many of whom were industrialists, military workers, government service men, businessmen, intellectuals, and ordinary citizens of the Ottoman Empire—were rounded up and killed. Men, women, and children died of starvation from marches across the Anatolian and Syrian desert plains.

The Cuban experience under Castro was also painful. It was on the wings of the hardships and political persecution that Raul's parents fled Cuba. As our families united by marriage, we had come to understand our common heritage of survival and there was an implicit bond of devotion that held us together. Synchronicity.

As Dad, Raul, my in-laws, and Mom entered the hospital, they were all directed to a small waiting room while I was transferred to intensive care. I was put under the care of the late Dr. Drue Neelley Ware and his team, who would watch over me for the next twelve days.

A doctor came out and told my family I was in a coma from the impact of the accident. I had been placed on a brain trauma protocol that included the lowering of my body temperature. The outcome was unknown, and the next twenty-four to forty-eight hours were critical in predicting my fate.

Raul and my family were given no assurances that I was going to survive. Eventually my Dad began asking the doctor questions. How long was I going to be in a coma? He was told it could be a few days or a few months. First, they had to make sure I would survive the initial impact, and for that the medical team would have to wait at least forty-eight hours. He said there were a number of complications, like brain swelling, internal bleeding, and more.

The doctor finally said, "She has to wake up within one week. If not, the damage will be deeper. The coma usually wins."

A little about me: People call me Kristin. Back in the days of living in Dhahran, Saudi Arabia, they would also call me "Saleri." They continued to do so in the years of living in Katy outside of Houston and all the way through college at Stephen F. Austin.

But I was also known as "Dawg" in high school. Who knows why, but I loved it.

During my elementary school years on the American compound in Dhahran, Saudi Arabia, my big brother, Sy, and I walked or cycled to and from school. Running out the front door and jumping on our bikes to head for school a mile away was an everyday normal. We studied hard, enjoyed two recesses per day (kickball was always a big deal), and went home for lunch, where Mom would have our food ready, specifically my favorite, buttered noodles. We would finish up class in the afternoon. Extra curriculars would take place after school. For me, that was swimming or soccer. Homework was just enough, as I could remember nothing too demanding. I remember doing a school project where the children had to invent brands of foods. Brother Sy came up with an idea to rename my cereal "Salerios" instead of "Cheerios."

A child couldn't have asked for a better place to grow up.

My favorite fourth grade teacher, Mrs. Draz, always wore navy or tan cotton skirts that reached her ankles. With her distinct olive skin, raspy voice, long brown hair, and freckly face, Mrs. Draz was sheepishly funny. She always had something clever to say when dismissing our class for the day. Her remarks would be followed by a poem from *Where the Sidewalk Ends* by Shel Silverstein. This was my all-time favorite book, with its cover etched with a black and white drawing of a boy, girl, and pup on the edge of an ending sidewalk. When Mrs. Draz would recite poems from *Where the Sidewalk Ends*, it was guaranteed to grab my attention.

One of the poems was titled, "Invitation," with lines that went: "If you are a dreamer, come in … For we have some flax-golden tales to spin." As she read, her ankle-length skirts swished about the school floors, accompanying the sounds of her soft raspy voice.

Dad worked for Aramco, the largest oil company in the world (also called the Saudi Oil Company) based out of Dhahran. He was a medium-built man with dark hair, dark eyes, and olive skin. He had a deep sounding voice that carried decibels in any environment. It functioned well at any competitive sports match like soccer, especially if he was coaching. He compared everything to soccer and still does to this day. For example, in response to something done by us children, he would say "yellow card!" "red card!" or "you're benched."

He was always in shape and loved to do his runs after a long workday. From a young age, I always admired my Dad's ethics both in work and play.

My parents arrived in the United States as two-week-old newlyweds in August 1970. Dad was pursuing graduate studies on a scholarship in chemical engineering at the University of Virginia. In his words, they came to America with $650, two suitcases, and lots of dreams! My brother, Sy, was born in 1972 and I was to follow on December 24, 1973. We were both born at Martha Jefferson Hospital, in the quaint college town of Charlottesville.

Mom was working as a librarian at the university. Working in the library was perfect for her, as it was always quiet, and she enjoyed helping students locate informative research and resources.

It was us four here in Charlottesville for our first three years of life. In 1978, Dad accepted a position in Los Angeles after he completed his PhD. Pauline, my sister, whom we call Popi, was welcomed to the world in Fullerton Hospital in Orange County, California.

At the hospital, Sy and I watched our baby sister from the window. Our attention was drawn to a lady going down the carpeted hallway. She was the first little adult we had ever seen. Her serious, tired expression matched her slow hobbling steps along the other side of the hall. She had grayish-brown hair and wore a long-sleeve, white shirt with a long skirt. She was hanging onto the railing against the wall. I was only four and a half years old then, and my instinct was to walk over, say hello, and lend her my helping hand. Looking back, I can say this was my earliest awareness of my instinctive need to care for others.

A month later we moved to Dhahran, Saudi Arabia, as my father had just accepted a foreign assignment with Chevron, where he was working as a research scientist with Saudi Aramco. Our perfectly settled family lived in a one-story, red-paneled house on a big corner lot. Well, it was big through the lens of a small child.

Yellow bars were propped up and embedded in the cement in front of the house.

The day I fell off of them, onto the black pavement, and broke my right forearm was a day to remember. I willingly went to the pool later that day with Sy and played my heart out with others in the pool. Although I knew something hurt, I wasn't sure that it would be broken. I hit the water with my forearm, splashing recklessly, trying to act as if there was no pain.

Later I learned I had broken my arm. The doctors quickly put on my cast using bandages and a milky-white glue that had to be slabbed on layer by layer. The doctor would wait until each layer would dry before placing the next. The stringent smell of pasty glue overtook the room. I wore that cast for six weeks at the age of six or seven. Even today as I inhale deeply, I can still smell the potency of the glue.

In Dhahran, our white picket fence was at the entrance of the pebbled walkway that led to the front door of our house, which was in the "main camp" as the Saudis called it. There was a main camp and then a nicer, upgraded area called the Dhahran Hills. If you headed out our gate onto the black concrete road and turned left up the cemented street, about a block away, you would walk through Mrs. Dara's gate and the entrance to her one-story house, our preschool.

Brother would walk me here every morning before he headed to Mrs. Chadwick's first grade class. Mrs. Dara's backyard was huge and filled with all the toys of a young child's dream. From monkey bars and rollaway cars to sandboxes and merry-go-rounds, everything fit perfectly in her spacious backyard. Every morning, Mom faithfully escorted Sy and I to the front of the picket fence and watched us go up the street to the preschool.

People in the Aramco community were always eating their shawarmas of luscious roasted meats wrapped in pita bread. This was a favorite Middle Eastern street food with things like hummus, tahini, pickles, vegetables, and even french fries added on. Besides feasting on yummy foods, the Aramco community was always finishing their shopping sprees in al-Khobar, a city located in the Eastern Province on the coast, before the prayer Adhan went off. The best shawarmas in all of Dhahran could be found at al-Khobar. At the time, women were still prohibited from driving, and this made outings for a Western woman more complicated, unless the man of the household was available to drive her after work or on the weekends.

The American compound where we lived stood in a seemingly never-ending desert landscape bordered by the Persian Gulf, or Arabian Sea, to the east, and the Red Sea to the west. We could run free on the compound for adventure. My favorite was our daily ATC rides. These were more dangerous three-wheeler models back in the early eighties. It was easier to roll off or flip over in comparison to the four-wheel ATVs, which are still highly risky to this day. Thank You God for keeping us safe in those days of riding the three-wheelers. Usually the pack included me, Leslie, Regina, Evelyn, and some of the guys (either of the two Jasons and Joey, if we were lucky, because he was older). All of these children had parents who worked in Aramco like mine, and we were sometimes called the Aramco Brats by outsiders who thought of us as pampered, entitled kids.

I remember that Evelyn, Leslie, Regina, and I once comprised what was Ms. Pengelly's fourth grade running group. Ms. Pengelly was one of our teachers. We once ran a race as one entity and finished together. We interlaced our hands and crossed the finish line of the "race" on a running trail of black pavement across from the Dhahran Hills Golf Course. Running was always a favorite activity of mine. The golf course at the time was made out of oil-treated sand. It looked like really dark-brown sand, as there was no vegetation that could grow in Dhahran's 120-degree heat in the summers. It made Houston feel like Anchorage, Alaska. The golf course is different now, as it's long been made into a green and luscious oasis.

Riding on ATCs all through the desert during the day, my friends and I still made sure to be home for our mothers' dinners. Mom's dolmas and BBQ chicken were among my favorites. She also had deliciously private ingredients for her "Mama/Nana Potatoes" as we've come to call them today.

On weekends you could find us snorkeling or sailing with friends in the beautiful coastal waters, or, in summertime, traveling the world with family.

Most of our elementary years were spent in our red house, until eventually, we moved to the "hills" as we called it, a few miles north of the compound. There were bigger homes here. Bigger homes, meaning the size of a town home. Our two-story town house was made of sandstone. Again, it was a short walk to the Dhahran Hills School, where I studied in second through fifth grade.

Swim team and soccer were our big to-dos at our young age. There was the Neptunes swim team for Sy, Popi, and I. Dad always coached Sy's soccer team. Sometimes I was lucky enough to play on the boys' soccer team! We wore maroon Charger jerseys, and my friend Megan and I played as hard as the boys. I was once guarding the goalpost and sure enough Mark Bowie was making the big kick for the goal and—*plow!*—his soccer-shoe cleat knocked my front tooth out. It was fair and square. My head just happened to be in the way of his perfect goal.

Blood poured everywhere, but like the broken arm, I was undaunted by the injury.

I wanted to keep playing, so did a quick wipe with a cloth the coach gave me.

I had the resilience of Hagopdede my grandfather, who had protected the family from the woes of the Armenian genocide.

Years later, Mom and Dad brought up the subject of moving to the States. Dad had accepted a Chevron job offer to return to Houston. He was excited by the professional prospects, and also, we as kids thought it was a great idea! Sy and I told our friends about our approaching adventure in the United States of America. The other Aramco kids would say,

"You're moving to the States?" "The United States!"

"So cool."

Everyone was so excited for us and our big move.

Plans were now underway. Not more than a year later, after I finished fifth grade, we were off to the U.S. "for good," as they would say in Dhahran. Once we said our farewells and Dad left the company, we were no longer allowed back into the Kingdom. The sad goodbyes to our best friends became an even sadder reality.

Our fine lives in Saudi soon became a memory. I honestly thought things would be okay and friends would be waiting for me with open arms in America. I never imagined the upcoming emotional struggle for my brother, sister (well, actually my sister was too young for it to faze her), and I, as well as for our parents.

The move happened in the summer of 1985, and it was a hard adjustment for me. Katy was a suburb of Houston, populated mainly with members of the nearby Baptist Church. It was not easy for freshly migrated parents of Armenian descent with children aged seven, eleven, and thirteen. For Sy and I, our preteen and teenage years were upon us in a new country.

It was a very lonely first three years in sixth, seventh, and eighth grades in Katy. Education wise, school was easier on the American compound in Dhahran, as our instruction was more personal and private. Dhahran was a very small community where everybody knew everybody. In contrast, everything in Texas was so, so huge. Everything was massive. At least the way I saw it as an eleven-year-old girl who had grown up in a tiny little American compound in Saudi Arabia.

My young mind kept wondering, *Why were things so different?* It seemed as though I was thrown into a sea of kids. Although I knew I was just an average student, my brother, sister, and I had thrived at the schools in Dhahran. I now wanted to go back to Dhahran. I missed my friends dreadfully, and I knew Sy was having as difficult a time as I was. But we would never tell this to our parents. I think, though, that Sy was a little more open about it than I was.

However, in high school things changed.

I gradually made friends who would stay with me for the rest of my life. The two Heathers, Erica, and Keely are still with me thirty years later. Actually, a whole group of our friends have stayed connected through all of our adult years, and we call ourselves the YaYa Sisterhood, based on the 1996 novel and later film starring Sandra Bullock. It turned out I would meet my husband, Raul, through Keely. Later we learned he'd also gone to the same high school as Heather Mahan. We were a close-knit circle of friends. It's always a small world, after all.

In 1992, the year I graduated from Taylor High School in Katy, my parents moved back to Saudi Arabia—my father had accepted a senior position with Aramco. They took my little sister, Popi, with them while I went to college in Nacogdoches and Brother was in San Francisco. As Saudi Arabia did not have tenth, eleventh, and twelfth grades, eventually Popi had to return for boarding school in the United States. She attended Brewster Academy in New Hampshire, which remains the nicest school I've ever seen in my life. It is surrounded by eighty acres of the

New England shoreline on Lake Winnipesaukee. One of my roommates and I would send her care packages frequently. I didn't understand why she was so homesick, being away from Saudi Arabia and my parents. With time, and as a parent now to a sixteen- and twenty-year-old, I came to understand that she was still young and tender at the age of sixteen. The distance from our parents had really set the brakes for her. Popi was feeling the natural vulnerability of a female teenager living far away from her parents.

During Popi's graduation, I recall that the actor John Lithgow gave the commencement address. His words inspired me to see the possibilities that our world has so much to offer.

Most of my friends graduated Stephen F. Austin about a semester before I did. However, new things were starting for me—I was engaged to be married. Invitations had been sent out for May 1998. I had found an exercise specialist job at Halliburton, where I was to organize gym workouts for the employees. I was twenty-three and ready for marriage and a family. Or I thought I was. As much as we like to think we have our life planned, God always seems to have the greater plans, right? Soon, though, I began to develop a nagging sensation of unease.

I needed something more. Sy was in San Francisco waiting tables as he grappled with academic and career options. Pauline eventually moved to Chicago to attend Lake Forest College after her time on the northeast coast. Meanwhile, I was neck deep in relationship challenges with my fiancé at the time. I realized that my impending marriage was not the best decision I had made.

After the broken engagement, my family had rallied around me, encouraging me and giving me the strength to look to brighter things.

I was lucky enough to always have supportive people around me. A healthy support system is the common denominator in getting through anything.

Back to the hospital where I lay, Memorial Hermann, the doctors eventually allowed my supportive army—my family—to visit me. But it would only be one person at a time and very, very seldomly. With the strict coma-management protocol, Dad deferred to the doctors.

It seemed to my family that there was a legion of doctors, which my Dad found particularly annoying to say the least. Probably only because it was a dire time for Mom and Dad. Every eight hours presented a different doctor who was very deliberate and guarded while describing my condition. A lot of unknown outcomes were cited. At the same time, they assured my family that everything medically possible was being done to save me.

"We're all hoping for a good outcome, but it's touch and go," repeated the doctors. "Touch and go" seemed to be their favorite phrase during this unknown time. As we talk about it today, those seemed to be the popular words used. "We're hoping that she's going to make it over the next twenty-four to forty-eight hours. However, there are quite a number of possible complications, including swelling of the brain, internal bleeding, and more."

Dad called his brother, Uncle Alen, with the unimaginable news. "Don't talk," Dad said. "Don't offer guidance. Just get on a plane and get here."

Some hours later, Uncle was in the waiting room. As a doctor, he had a terrible feeling the moment he saw my MRI. As he would tell me later, to decode a brain MRI could take years, but not when you see a cerebellum neatly split in half. He instantly felt shivers down his spine as his doctor's mind kicked in: Kristin would never walk again. Kristin would forever be confined to a wheelchair. And that of course would be good luck, for she may not even survive.

"Am I wrong to think the cerebellum is injured?" Uncle asked the radiologist, who also had his eyes locked on my brain image. The sterile medical office mimicked what the radiologist was about to report. He was silent for a few seconds and then said, "This is not good."

Did Uncle hear his response? Yes.

Did anything register? No.

Uncle's body was now on fire, as he reported to me years later, and he had waves of nausea. He said he felt his guts were in charge, then he quickly surrendered to pain and helplessness and the best thing he could do was pray. He said there was no room for doctoring as a bystander.

The realization set in with my family that they had to have a longer-term plan of more than forty-eight hours—there were no straight answers about my situation and what the lasting consequences of my comatose state would be. These were not the topics the doctors wanted to discuss in the early hours of extreme crisis. Eventually, my family was advised that my recovery was going to be a long journey and that they would have to take care of themselves as well.

The family organized a rotational support program. They took turns entering the ICU to talk to my unconscious body. They were up days and nights, never wavering. Raul was allowed to see me more often though, and the family respected that. Raul would hold my hand everyday while reading novels and talking to me. "Please Kristin, you can do this; you got this. Jacob and I love you so much and need you." Raul would recite the Lord's Prayer and any other prayer that came to mind.

I still had bleeding and hemorrhaging in the brain and was making strange noises. Lying there, in the intensive care unit at Memorial Hermann, I was in and out of consciousness. I was still unaware of what was happening. I had very vivid dreams. Dreams of color. Dark navy hues, ocean hues. I once saw myself on the lower level of a ship, looking out of a porthole at the night sky. I saw navy-blue choppy waves crashing against themselves. They appeared like the dark waters of my swim in San Francisco Bay, in the Alcatraz Challenge that foggy Sunday morning. Or it could have been the Marmara Sea frothing beneath the ferry from Istanbul to Burgaz Island. A few weeks prior to the accident, we had taken a trip to Istanbul to visit family, so I could've been reliving that memory in the dreams of my coma.

Whatever it was, it seemed I was in an enclosed room on the ship or ferry. The room was crammed with a bed or two, with barely any space. In and out of consciousness, I heard the nurses talking to one another. I would make some weak sounds or say random words to which they replied by asking me questions or reassuring me.

Where was I?

I would hear Father Drew, the family parish priest, calling my name. "Kristin, Kristin, Kristin." It was a soft voice, almost a whisper.

I opened my eyes. I must have woken from a nap. *It is such a joy to see him, as a feeling of peace radiated my body. How sweet; this is so nice. Moments such as this should happen more often...*

I closed my eyes again, sliding back into the world of crashing waves and a faraway night sky.

By the third day I had lost so much blood that I was in desperate need of an O-positive blood transfusion. The doctors restabilized my system after the transfusion, but I was yet to regain a wakeful state. I remained in both a natural and medically induced coma brought on by the controlled administration of barbiturates. This procedure was done only in cases of extreme trauma in order to reduce the amount of energy needed by brain function, eventually healing swelling and protecting areas previously at risk.

The main thing about a drug-induced coma as opposed to a natural coma is that it is reversible. If a barbiturate-induced coma were to be introduced to someone with a normal, functioning brain, they would come right out of the coma once the drugs were stopped. In my case, I had yet to come out of mine.

On the morning of day seven, my father was sitting by my bedside and talking to my still body, when I suddenly turned to him and asked, "Dad, what's the scoop?" I was so loud and clear that Dad was stunned. He shouted, "Oh my God, Kristin! You woke up!"

He ran out of the room and announced to everyone that I had woken up!

My mother and Raul came in to see for themselves, but I had fallen asleep again. They were on either side of my hospital bed. They talked to me while fixing my pillows and blankets. My face was turned to Mom's side of the room.

"I want to go home," I mumbled.

Mom was overwhelmed. She jumped for joy. "Raul, she just spoke!"

"No," my husband answered. "I didn't hear her."

"Raul," Mom said, "she wants to go home. She says she wants to go home."

"No, no," he replied.

"But no! I heard her," Mom exclaimed. "She mumbled it and I heard her because I was right there, and her head was turned toward me. She said, 'I want to go home,' like that!"

Those were my first words to Raul and Mom, but I don't remember. I'd drifted off again.

My husband's reaction was understandable. He had a one-and-a-half-year-old at home. His spouse was in a coma. He had heavy responsibilities at work. Here was a guy trying to do whatever needed to be done in order to make a living for his family; and then his wife gets hit by a car going twenty-five miles an hour. A lot had to be running through his head at the time.

But I had woken up on the seventh day and it was big news! The joy spread to all the Cubans and Armenians in the waiting room. Both Maky and Pauline say that when they spoke to one of the doctors in charge, he mentioned me as having a 90 percent recovery chance if I woke up. Well, I did wake up, and they became worried because, in their words, it was five minutes up and then I would fall deep asleep again.

Each time I awakened, the nurse would come out and tell the family, "She's awake," and somebody would go in. But right after, I would fall into deep sleep again.

With time, as I started coming awake more often, it was hard for me to understand what all this meant because I didn't even know I was in the hospital. When I could stay awake for longer periods, I was transferred to a second ICU unit where the nurses would sit me up and stabilize me with belts, or else I would fall back onto the bed like a doll without a spine.

I tried to walk and was helped out of bed. The nurses surrounded me. A belt was tied around me for support and Raul, Dad, and Mom were cheering me on. Why are they cheering me on? I wondered. I sensed it was a big deal that I was walking but didn't know why. I remember looking down at the white, speckled floor tiles and wondering why I was unable to walk. *Why is this so hard for me? Why?*

I knew I had to do it, but I also knew how hard it was, without knowing why.

My mind was unaware of the gravity of the situation.

It was very encouraging that I was able to move my legs, but it was also emotional for my family to see me walking the way I was, like a raggedy doll.

It was shortly after I began walking that the doctors cleared me to be transferred to TIRR (The Institute of Rehabilitation and Research). This was on October 12, 2002. At that point, the nurses and caretakers loaded me onto a gurney and placed me in the ambulance to TIRR. They dropped me off in the circle driveway—at least I remember it as a circle driveway. The ambulatory care wheeled me up to the second floor, which was the brain-injury floor at TIRR.

My small room had white walls. A white board was affixed opposite my bed, where the nurses would write my daily schedules. There was a ledge and an off-white linen curtain behind the board to separate my space from that of my roommates.

A small television was also set in the corner. Raul and Pauline would catch episodes of *The Bachelorette* and I would sometimes watch along with them. Next to my twin bed was a blue-vinyl tow-armed chair along with a shelf. The bathroom was a few feet away. It had a shower and toilet with arm bars. A low chair was placed in the white-walled shower for handicap ease. Everything was handicap friendly.

"Mom, what's going on?" I later asked my mother.

She was folding my clothes or had grabbed something from the chair. "You were hit by a car," Mom softly and calmly responded, as though I was going to react somehow.

I didn't understand. I tried to make sense of her response to me, but it made no sense at all, especially since my memory had gaps from that beautiful, sunny day. The last thing I remembered was the dinner at Perry's Italian place.

I thought, "Here we go. She's overreacting again. Why is she talking as if this is a life-changing event or something?"

What was wrong with everybody?

In my mind, nothing was adding up.

Later, I got up to walk to the bathroom just a short distance from me. I couldn't lift my body. My legs wouldn't support me.

Raul's father, Buelo, was sitting in the chair next to my bed.

"Will you give me a hand?" I asked.

"Safety first," said Buelo, as he shot to his feet. He nervously whipped his head around and then called outside the room for a nurse to assist me. Again, I would say to myself, what is going on with everyone?

Slowly but surely, I started realizing life was now different. When I would ride a recumbent bike for ten minutes, with a physical therapist acting as if I was a child, I would think, *What the heck? Does she know I'm way ahead of this? Does she know I was training for a marathon and can do more? Why is she making me do the recumbent bike for only ten minutes, and I have to beg for twenty?*

I kept pedaling, thinking, *Why are people cheering me on for doing basic things? Oh boy, I have to let them know it's okay to let me be my own coach.*

This was a new stage for me. A new life.

But all I wanted was to be home. I wanted to be with Raul and my little Jacob again.

I missed my family.

6

Motherhood

Jacob saw me shortly before my transfer to TIRR, on my last day at Memorial Hermann. Since his pediatrician thought it would be traumatic for him to see his mother trickling with tubes and hooked up to machines, it was decided that I had to move on to a more "normal-looking" mode before my baby could see me. But I asked about Jacob every day, from the moment I woke up.

One day, when Maky was in the room with Raul, she pointed to my husband and asked, "Do you know who this is?"

I said, "Raul," then immediately, "Jacob, Jacob," before falling back to sleep. My mind had associated Raul with our baby.

When Jacob finally got to see me, it was likely emotional for him to see me in that setting, but we can't know all that goes on in a child's mind. Oh, how I wish we could. It must've been so hard for a one-and-half-year-old who hadn't seen his mommy in however many weeks.

What had he been feeling when his mom abruptly vanished from his life? I wish I could have gotten in his head. Did he notice that I was gone at barely two years old?

Martha, Raul's sister, had placed him on my bed. I kept trying to bring him closer. My body would not let me. I couldn't move; I couldn't even hold myself up. Everything felt like mush, although I was propped up in bed to look normal. My small nephews in the room moved at lightning speed compared to me. I felt ambushed by overwhelming feelings of sadness at not being able to join in the fun and only smile at them, watching from a distance. I had zero control and this feeling was so foreign to me. Where had I been? What happened?

The shooting pain down my arm would not let me grasp Jacob. My broken ribs didn't let me hug or laugh with him, either. I watched the cousins play, and when I would attempt a laugh, an excruciating pain diffused through my right side. Even taking a deep breath would hurt. I made a note to self to move slightly, since any turning would agitate the hell out of my chest. At the same time, my broken scapula was screaming. I would compare it all to a red-hot sledgehammer pounding my side, arm, and upper back.

My broken tailbone didn't help the situation either. It felt like a dull sword poking out of my lower back. Raul had placed many pillows behind me to keep me in an upright position. My eyes were the only thing that took me places. However, it hurt to look at things. I could see two Jacobs and two of everything else in the room. This was the double vision, or diplopia, caused by the forceful impact to my optic neurons. Squinting became a fast friend of mine in order to gain focus on a given moment. For the time being, the doctors had me wear a black patch, or sunglasses if I had to momentarily remove the patch. My eye issue would not go away until I had corrective surgery one year later. Everything was double. As time moved forward, I learned to get used to it. I successfully learned the tricks of the trade, to manage with one eye or to close one eye when doing things.

Touching Jacob's little body was enough to keep me full for the moment.

As fast as the family entered my hospital room, they left. It was short and sweet. Doctors must have instructed them to keep it a short and simple visit.

I peacefully dozed off. My brain was calling for rest. My system had to get back to the job of repairing injured cells.

Later, Jacob would ask me, "Mommy, did you get a boo-boo?"

"Yes, honey, but everything's okay," I'd say.

Touching him for the first time after I woke up reminded me of the hours following his birth, when I first held him after both our fevers had subsided following an eighteen-hour labor and emergency C-section. I'd hugged all eight pounds and eleven ounces of him to my breast. Those early days at Memorial Hermann and TIRR brought back the old feelings of lost time with my baby and the things that could have been.

Raul and I were still in the early stages of dating when life came at us with a surprise pregnancy. After we met, we knew we were falling in love, but I knew to take things slow as well. We were compatible when it came to faith and values, and I'd assumed we would wait until marriage to have sex.

One day, as we were in the middle of a conversation, Raul, then boyfriend, said to me—and I shall never forget the way he said it because he was carefully counting on his fingers— "One, two, three, four, five. We've been dating for five months, Kristin." He looked at me with his brown eyes, his Hershey Kisses.

I sensed I would ultimately marry him. But little did we know that when we made passionate love for the first or second time, Jacob would be created, thus throwing open the doors for a marriage plan sooner than we would have expected.

We got pregnant with Jacob in March 2000.

At first, I didn't know I was pregnant. I'd started feeling sick, had lost my appetite, and didn't know what was wrong with me. Raul was concerned and bought a pregnancy test kit. "You need to take this test," he kept telling me, even though I thought I had a vicious stomach bug of some sort. As these are sure signs of pregnancy my mind was stuck on the stomach bug. I thought that there was no way I could be pregnant.

I was on my way to work when he bought the kit, I just grabbed it and I put it in my nylon Nike backpack. As soon as I had a break between patients at work, I used the kit in the restroom and put it back in my backpack without looking. Pregnancy was the furthest thing from my mind. Meanwhile, Raul had a golf tournament in the Woodlands later that day, and while he was in the midst of a game, I remembered the kit and looked into my backpack.

And I saw it. I saw two lines.

"Hmm."

I read the instructions on the back of the kit and immediately went into complete panic. I started bawling hysterically. I called Raul from the office. I can't remember whether I had a patient or not.

If I did, I had probably made the patient walk on the treadmill while I was in the office talking to Raul.

At the sound of my weepy voice he asked, "What's wrong?"

"What do you think is wrong?" I cried.

"I'll be right there," he said.

I rushed home and had my friend Heather meet me there. I broke down with the news. She consoled me and tried to make me see sense in talking it out with Raul. I recall I had a happy hour planned with colleagues that afternoon but had to cancel. My world was spinning out of control, and I was in shock.

The doorbell rang as Heather was exiting. Raul had arrived at my apartment with cookies from Paulie's restaurant. They were my favorite cookies, best cookies ever. I wasn't prepared for what happened next. He brought out a ring from his jeans pocket and looked at me intently. Forever was happening.

"Will you marry me?" he asked. "Yes," I said immediately.

He didn't tell me until years later that he had sold his entire stock portfolio to purchase the ring.

We had a lot to talk about. We were afraid of this unexpected circumstance, but we both knew we wanted to keep the baby. But marriage? Was I ready for that? Were we ready for that?

Gosh, things were happening so fast.

We decided to announce our engagement, and it was agreed that our baby would be named Jacob after my paternal grandfather, Hagopdede.

I had to call my parents from eight thousand miles away. This was not the way I ever imagined I would tell them, but we were ready to share the news. I debated about who to first give the news to, Mom or Dad.

Dad picked up the phone.

"Dad, will you put Mom on the phone?"

It was on a Thursday, which was a weekend in Saudi Arabia. This was right in the middle of their dinner—an unusual day and time for me to call, as I normally called on Sundays to hail my father with the greeting, "Dad, what's the scoop?"

This time I didn't greet Dad in the usual way. He knew something was wrong. In important matters I would first seek his opinion; now I was making it clear that this case was outside his territory. Dad passed the phone to Mom and picked up another extension at the end of the house, listening. Thinking I was talking to just my mother, I told her that I was pregnant.

She was silent at first.

The silence continued...

"How could you go and do something like that?" she asked.

I honestly didn't know how to respond. I didn't quite know the answer myself. I took a deep breath and took a big sip of my Dr. Pepper.

"I don't know, Mom. I love him, that's all I know. We're getting married in July," I said. I was sitting on my brown floral couch in midtown, off West Dallas Street. I was wearing my workout clothes. I actually was in disbelief too, and I placed my hand on my cheek. I quickly stood up and started pacing nervously in the kitchen as we said our goodbyes and love yous to end the call. Just then Rachael happened to shout my name from the balcony above—she lived directly upstairs, and we were always conversing from our patios.

I was twenty-five, pregnant, and getting married in two months, in July. Yes, I did love him; but it had been a short courtship lasting seven months by this time. Thank God Mom remembered me talking about him in Istanbul, when we were there for the millennial new year.

Looking back, it breaks her heart now that she said what she said. I know she was reacting out of motherly love and instinct, as I was her first-born daughter. What mother wouldn't respond like that? In addition, my call was further confirmation of a dream she'd had the night before. Mom said that in it I was a little girl again, and she was throwing me in the air and catching me.

This was the setting in which my parents were introduced to Raul. About a week later, they had a phone conversation with him. Dad was, rightfully, full of questions and concerns. This was his eldest daughter, and he had no earthly idea who Raul was. As it turned out, it was a short conversation, lasting maybe three or four minutes. But in that brief time, my Dad was convinced Raul was the right person for me. His confidence, his assured way, the honesty with which he expressed himself, and especially Raul's recognition of the circumstances and all the challenges we faced, was very impressive to my Dad.

Raul totally understood my father's anxiety. At the end of their conversation, Dad said he felt that Raul was the right person for me because, although I had a history of dating some other very nice young men, none had given him the confidence that Raul gave him in that three-minute conversation. There was something different about Raul, and Dad would say that difference was his honesty.

Dad likens my personality to that of a cat, as he thinks I have a very quick way of figuring out who's right and who's wrong. That also played into Dad's thinking: If I was so convinced that Raul was the right person, then that was something to be said about the subject. Now, years later, both Mom and Dad say they are very fortunate to have Raul as, essentially, another son within the family.

The planning of the wedding started. It was an expedited summer wedding on the fifteenth of July 2000. We planned it in six weeks, and our lives have been on fast-forward ever since. Our beautiful ceremony was held at Sacred Heart Co-Cathedral Catholic Church in downtown Houston, where the divinely painted face of Jesus stared at us from above the altar as we took our vows.

My ivory satin wedding dress was topped with a white cathedral veil that draped gently over my back. I modeled my gorgeous freshwater pearls, which outlined my neckline. They were a gift from Mom, and their splendor was so artful and matched my joyous mood.

"Ava Maria" was sung by our family friend, Beba. Her voice echoed beautifully throughout the church; then one by one the wedding party went down the aisle. Seven of my nearest and dearest friends and cousins radiated beauty in their soft champagne bridesmaid's dresses. Four were dear friends from college—Keri, Jamie, April, and Jeri—while the other two were dear friends from childhood—Heather Gunn and Heather Mahan. My dear little sister, Popi, and soon to be sisters, April and Martha, were part of the train, which included my one and only junior bridesmaid, Chloe.

There was my handsome nephew, Daniel, with his dirty-blonde hair, so fashionable in his ivory-colored ring-bearer attire. Daniel's white socks were pulled up perfectly to his knees. His parents had bribed him—if he walked down the aisle like a little gentleman, with no tears, they would get him a goldfish. Whatever it takes! Ha, it worked. Chloe, my nine-year-old cousin, with her skinny, yet athletic build, was boldly walking ahead. She personified our Armenian heritage. Wearing her beautiful white gown, Chloe's soft and light brunette hair was perfectly pulled back. Her bouquet of ivory blossomed roses was held elegantly in her hands.

I held my overpoweringly beautiful, ornate, yellow- and ivory-hued bouquet of roses. They were eye gripping, as they were perfectly freshly picked and blossomed. As the wedding march elegantly began playing on the piano, Dad locked his arm with mine. The church silenced as everyone's faces turned toward me. I smiled widely and felt a rush of nervous energy come over me; butterflies started in my stomach, too, at this point. Dad and I walked our way down the aisle, and I gleamed with happiness, knowing that it was Raul at the end, calmly waiting for me at the altar.

Dad kissed my cheeks on both sides, then turned and gently gave my hand to Raul. He looked so handsome in his black tuxedo and ivory bow tie, which complimented the ivory rose boutonniere on his lapel.

Father Tom said, in a joyful but serious tone, "Raul and Kristin, have you come here freely and without reservation to give yourselves to each other in marriage? Will you honor each other as man and wife for the rest of your lives? Will you accept children lovingly from God and bring them up according to the law of Christ and his church?" He knew I was pregnant and that we were eager to bring our baby into this world together. Hearing the words, immediately we said, "I do."

During the vows my mouth felt extra dry, and Pauline kept having to get me water. Sometimes Father Tom would look at me and ask if I was okay. Of course, I was, I was only excited and nervous. As we all gathered for photographs, a dizzy feeling overtook me, and I swooned to the floor.

Trying to catch myself, my uncle came to the rescue. Immediately, he ran to the altar, threw me over his shoulder and hurried all the way to the limo outside. Personally, I wished he hadn't thrown me over his shoulder. I didn't want guests to notice such a dramatic scene. Inside the car, I lay silently as I took deep breaths while Uncle took my pulse. I was feeling sheepishly embarrassed. Fainting at my own wedding, did that really just happen? All I needed was hydration and to loosen this dress. I had gotten my wedding dress fitted extra tight that morning in the bid to not look pregnant at my own wedding. Bad idea!

Raul immediately hopped in the limo, and we drove to the reception venue at the Houstonian Hotel, where Mom met me at the entrance. She turned into an immediate seamstress as she unbuttoned six back buttons and tucked the flaps under on both the left and right sides. It looked seamless. She magically transformed the fitted dress and saved the day.

The reception was held at the hotel's The Manor House, a historic home designed in 1955 by renowned architect John Staub. It was a beautiful outdoor, summer reception with the band playing under a lit white tent to create an intense ambiance. The perfectly manicured green lawn led all the guests to the white tent. The Manor House, where U.S. President George H.W. Bush and First Lady Barbara Bush would frequently dine, was the venue of my dreams.

Sy was having a great time being the live entertainment as the MC for the evening. Mom smiled at me from afar.

Raul and I began our dance by staring into one another's eyes and feeling our eternal love as the band played Billy Joel's classic tune "She's Always a Woman."

Dad and I had a hearty laugh as we danced to "Wind Beneath My Wings" by Bette Midler.

Thanking our guests, Raul and I danced our way out as we were showered by rose petals from family and friends. The celebration continued into the late hours of the evening.

For our honeymoon, we were off to the Cayman Islands. There, our favorite time was beach time. At sixteen-weeks pregnant, my body just relaxed after arriving in the Caymans. I ate and drank everything alcohol free. It was during this time that I expanded; it was great timing. Jacob started growing in abundance. I gained a lot of weight after the wedding—thanks, Jacob! Fortunately, there was no morning sickness. I was in great health and ran until the week before his birth.

Jacob was born on December 18, 2000. The accident was twenty-one months later.

Our story, with the surprise pregnancy and expedited wedding, was a love story.

Raul was true to the vows he made to me at the altar on that hot summer day in July. From the beginning of our journey as a family, he was not going to leave my side, and he proved himself during my catastrophic accident.

From the beginning, Dad, in first meeting Raul and talking to him, told him not to underestimate the element of "wildness" in me, as he likes to describe it. Dad thinks I've always been a free spirit who brought a lot of energy, excitement, exuberance, and unpredictability into my relationship with Raul. On the other hand, Raul brought wisdom, stability, calm, reliability, and a certain coolness. Dad recognized early on that it was a combination that worked.

Raul and my family were with me for Jacob's birth. I remember the day—it was a long day with a long labor. In fact, in the middle of the labor the doctor told us the baby was not arriving anytime soon, and we were to return home and come back when I was more dilated. I felt it was a case of false labor, so our caravan returned back home. Of course, I was naturally annoyed, going back and forth on the bumpy roads in Houston at thirty-nine weeks pregnant.

At home, I turned on the bath and tried to relax. But I knew it was happening. *Why did they send me back home?* I thought. After all, there was a reason I had gone to the hospital in the first place. Then it happened.

"Raul, we have to go, my water broke!" I called.

I was now sure of it, there was no guessing on that one. We all jumped in cars and raced in a caravan back to Memorial City Hospital. It was past midnight, or around one in the morning, when Mom almost got a speeding ticket because she made a turn where she shouldn't have. She had to explain to the cop that she'd made the turn because I was in labor. The Houston police officer was very understanding and gave her a pass.

In the maternity ward I developed a fever during my intense eighteen-hour labor. I was no longer dilating. The on duty maternity nurse said, "If you have so much fever, the child must be burning. We should deliver the baby immediately." She was talking with her hands, and her long fingernails waved in the air.

In my feverish mind her fingernails overtook the conversation. I wanted to cry. Maybe I did. Is she really saying this and checking me with her lengthy nails? This cannot be up to par by hospital standards. I was at her mercy—she was my nurse, and my fever was escalating. At that point, the nurses wheeled me into the operating room. The doctor performed an emergency C-Section and Jacob was welcomed to the world.

Shortly after the accident, one day my mother-in-law, Maky, came into my hospital room to find me half-awake. I don't remember how many days I had been out of the coma, but I looked at Maky and called her "Viya," a family term of endearment for her. It was a nickname made up by my nephew, Daniel, and it has carried through to today. Before the accident I had always called her Viya.

Once I called her by that nickname, Maky said she knew I was going to make it.

Then I asked her for a toothbrush to brush my teeth. When Maky recounted the story, Raul and my parents laughed and said, "That's Kristin."

My recovery was a slow and steady process. At the beginning the nurses would ask who the president was and what time it was. It was their morning protocol to ask basic questions. Then one day I quipped to the nurse, "How about you look behind you? There's a clock on the wall." When Pauline told me how I responded, embarrassment overtook me, especially saying something like that to someone who was trying to help me.

Knowing me, I think I was getting sick of being asked those basic questions.

"It was your humor that got us through it all," Sister would always say.

7

Healing

If you were to ask my father, he'd say that I was entertaining from the day I was born. Unlike most babies, I was born with a smile and not a cry and was also very beautiful—but those are his words, not mine. I reminded him very much of his mother, whose tenacity and drive I inherited. He referred to me as "The Angel" as I grew up, but that quickly changed when I became a teenager and a different type of personality emerged. A good word for it would be wild—the high side of normal teenage behavior.

I was very rebellious in everything and tested my parents' ability to manage me. They decided that I was uncontrollable and did their best to tolerate me in the hopes that I would eventually grow into a nice, productive woman. However, in my defense, drugs were never part of the equation. To me, I was a regular teenager doing regular teenage things, growing up in the USA as first generation. I may not have clear memories of how and when those "wild" things, as Dad puts them, happened. But Dad does. He remembers a lot actually.

Such as, in 1992, my parents made a decision that coincided with me going to Stephen F. Austin State University as a freshman. They had to move back to Saudi Arabia because Dad was to assume a management position with Saudi Aramco. I had spent my first seven years as a child there, and, as my parents relocated there, I made it a point to visit twice a year, typically for Christmas and summer. As sad as I was that my parents were moving back to Saudi, I was also feeling happy and very free—how new high school graduates imagine themselves to be so independent and are unaware that, in reality, they are still kids. Scientists always state that the frontal lobe is not fully developed until the age of twenty-five or so. All executive functioning takes place here, from cognitive thinking to planning and organizing. Basically, anyone less than this age is not an adult; neurologically, no one is fully prepared for adulthood until this age.

So, on that Christmas of 1992, I arrived in Dhahran for my regular visit. I was very happy. My parents, who came to pick me up at the airport, looked shocked as I was walking out of customs. I couldn't understand the confusion and distress on their faces. All I had on my mind was boyfriends, parties, and college social life. My parents were appalled at the fact that I was wearing khaki shorts in a Saudi Arabian airport! Dad said I wore a mile-long smile on my face all the while, oblivious to the fact that the Saudi men were in a frenzy. The Mutawas, or religious police, could not only arrest me for indecent public behavior but arrest my father as well, and kick him out of the country.

As a follow-up, a few weeks later my family was attending a social gathering in Dhahran with some friends. A man my parents just met began telling a story that went, "Two weeks ago I was at the airport. I couldn't believe it, but can you believe, for the first time in Dhahran, there was this young woman who came out wearing shorts, and all the Saudi men were in a frenzy. Can you believe this is happening in Dhahran?"

And my wonderful Dad calmly replied, "I happen to be the father of that girl."

We still laugh about that story today.

Dad also recalls another significant one from my Stephen F. Austin college years. I would have weekly telephone calls with my parents, who worried about my academics. They wanted to make sure I was staying on course and would graduate on time. Another point of concern was my financial well-being because Dad thought me a bit excessive with expenditures. I had to manage my budget, live within my means, and not abuse the credit-card privileges I'd been given.

However, my father recalls receiving an interesting letter from me one day. It was a birthday card along with a thank-you card and a long note. I was thanking him for being a fantastic father and wishing him nice things for his birthday. But that was not all. There was also a check for $600, which my father didn't understand because I had a monthly allowance. So, he read the note attached to the check. It said: "Dad, I want you to know that I'm going to Hawaii this summer with a friend of mine." (The friend was Jamie, a sorority sister.) The note continued:

> We are actually going to take a credited course,
> that counts toward graduation, in golfing. And I
> already purchased the tickets on your Mastercard
> for Jamie and me ... and I already paid for the
> tuition. Of course, I realize I shouldn't be paying
> for my friend's ticket and golfing course on your
> account, but I promise to pay you over the next
> four months.

To make a long story short, I had billed my father's account for about $3,000. The $600 check was the first-installment payback plan.

Dad thought it was ingenious—very well-conceived and executed—because I had already gone to Hawaii by then. Thus, this was after the deed was done. I wasn't really asking for his permission.

Anyway, I did pay back all of the money I owed Dad. But we still have different versions to this day about what really happened. To my recollection, I hadn't paid for Jamie's trip and even borrowed money from her while in Hawaii. I was so out of money that I would go to the Chevron station and offer to pay for people's gas using Dad's Chevron card in exchange for cash. It was a college student's dream to get cash for filling up gas. My parents were not pleased when they later found out about my Chevron card tricks but Jamie always tells me her grandfather, the late Tex Schramm, general manager of the Dallas Cowboys, thought it was ingenious of me! I loved getting compliments from successful grandparents who had been there and done that.

Jamie and I had long days of touring Honolulu and laying on Waikiki Beach after golf class in the morning. We did know that our parents gave us the privilege to have this opportunity of travel and made sure we lived our time here to the fullest, especially seeing all the historic sites in the area. We took the windiest road in Hawaii up the mountain to black beaches, where we enjoyed the salty air from the Pacific and watched the violet Maui sunsets. Bar hopping was our favorite to-do. Ironically, I was carrying the very same nylon backpack that later held Jacob's pregnancy test kit. I was even wearing the same ball cap as on the day of my accident years later.

Despite all of this, my father is, and continues to be, the one who describes me with the most grace and charm. We have a friendship more than a father-daughter relationship.

In the manner of his stories about me, Dad would recall that first week in the intensive care unit at Memorial Hermann as exceptional. As I've previously said, every member from both sides of my family came into the ward to talk to my comatose form during the first seven days. It was their daily routine—everyone took turns in ones or twos. They would come in and make loving statements.

Dad would say, "Kristin, we love you. You're going to come out. Please wake up, marathon girl. You can do it."

Mom would say, "Kristin, please wake up. The worst is behind us. You're going to do it."

Dad has shared that there are certain heavy-hearted moments in life—perhaps a dozen of them—that rise above every other in a person's lifetime. One such moment for him was waking my mother to tell her about the accident on that day. Another moment was on the Sunday, the seventh day, following the accident. After a refreshing shower at the hotel, he thought this was the day my waking up from the coma had to happen.

When he came into the ICU and sat by me, he said, "Kristin, marathon girl, I want you to wake up. Today is the seventh day. I want you to wake up."

Suddenly, I turned to Dad and said, "Dad, what's the scoop?" It was as if a bolt of lightning went through my father. "Kristin, my God, you woke up! I can't believe this. This is incredible."

"Dad, what's the scoop?" I repeated, loud and clear as if nothing had happened.

It was our usual opening greeting. Dad said I was so clear and firm in my voice that it totally shocked him. It even shocks me to hear this eighteen years later. To date, Dad continues to tell the story of me saying these words on waking up, but I have no recollection of this. Actually, I don't even remember the background of this greeting anymore. But hearing this story continues to warm my heart.

"Kristin, don't worry about it!" Dad said. "You were involved in a bad accident. Thank God, God gave you back to us. Everything is going to be okay." He was under the impression that I was processing everything that he was telling me. Unbeknownst to him, my consciousness was just a momentary thing. I was still coming out of the coma, but not back to my conscious, wild-Kristin mode.

But my father was in Heaven. He ran out of the room and screamed to Raul and my mother, "She woke up! She's out of the coma! She woke up ... she's out of the coma!"

Later, on the same day, Mom and Raul were in the room when I turned toward Mom and softly said, "Let's go home."

Mom said, "Raul, she said something. She said, 'Let's go home.'"

"No way," Raul replied, because he couldn't hear me. Mom said, "I'd know if she said it. She just said it."

I fell right back to sleep.

Raul, Mom, and Dad were the first people to see me wake up from the coma.

Other people came in, but they didn't get the same type of response from me as Raul, Mom, and Dad had gotten. But the medical personnel confirmed that I was waking up, that I was talking. I wasn't exactly coherent, but my speaking was an encouraging sign.

It was Sunday. It was day seven.

As they'd been told by the doctor, any coma exceeding seven days could lead to worse brain damage and even a vegetable state.

Seven days is biblical. By day seven, God finished his work of creation and rested, making the seventh day a special holy day. As it happened, seven was Dad's favorite number as well. Brother Sy's birthday, too. He was born on the 7th of April.

Now that I had woken up, my family was confident that I would beat all odds, that I was going to recover, that life would be great again.

I happened to be an outlier by God's divine intervention. After roughly ten days, I began to take a more vertical position in bed. I was able to slightly move my arms and legs. Eventually, the doctors wanted me to stand up and take a few steps with assistance. I wobbled like a tree in the wind and had no control of my bottom extremities. The crash had hit on the cerebellum part of the brain which was responsible for balance, coordination, and walking.

The benchmark was three or four steps at the beginning. Three nurses supported me, one on each side and one behind me. I was using a device with a girdle strap and a wheeled adult walker. Mom was with us. Raul walked beside me. I was Jacob taking his first steps at nine months, except he was running at nine months, and it came naturally to him. This was my second time around, twenty-eight years later, and things were not as easy.

I was determined and took about fifty steps. Dad, who was helping, said he could see the pain in my face. He knelt on the floor a few feet away and cheered me on. "Kristin, you can do it. One more step," he said encouragingly.

Given Dad's vocal power when he roots for his favorite teams, the whole hospital could hear him cheering and crying as he rallied me to take one more step, one more step, one more step.

My first walk after the accident has left an unforgettable impression on us all.

Shortly after, I got moved into a private room for about a day or two before I was finally transferred to TIRR.

Dr. Gerard Francisco, now Chief Medical Officer at TIRR Memorial Hermann, was ultimately to be my doctor at TIRR. He was actually the first doctor that I could remember. It could also be that he holds a place in my heart because he shared the same name as the city that I loved, where my brother lived and where I had raced in the Alcatraz Challenge—San Francisco. Although I didn't realize it at the time, it was nothing short of synchronicity. I knew that since I had maneuvered the physical barriers of the rock at Alcatraz, I was sure to get past this rock of relearning life.

In the meantime, there were a lot of complications to deal with. I had an undetected source of internal bleeding and faced several complications as a result. When I awoke from the coma, the complications miraculously lessened, then vanished. While at TIRR, Maky recalls me sleeping almost all day. She once said to Dr. Francisco, "Can you wake her up?" And he replied, "I'm not waking her up." The doctor preferred to work with my body's pace. He believed my waking from the coma was a feat, so it was best to let my body set its own rhythm.

I was soon riding the recumbent bike a minute a day, then five minutes, and on to ten. Baby steps it was to the new normal. I also remember working with some blue balance balls. There were benchmarks for recovery, like putting on your shirt or brushing your teeth. I had occupational therapy sessions, physical therapy, speech therapy, every type of therapy that one could imagine. It was a detailed schedule that I followed.

One interesting thing with TIRR was that you didn't have your own room. The first person I shared a room with was a lady who had suffered a stroke while giving birth. I remember that she and her husband were usually quiet and peaceful. The "normal me" would have been friendly and asked how I could be of help to them. But at this point in my recovery, I had no energy to do so. It all had been sucked out of me, trying to be human again. One evening, my phone fell on the tiled floor with a loud crash and the husband immediately called out, "Are you okay?"

"Yes," I replied, "thanks."

The second person was a sweet, older lady who fell and hit her head while riding a bike. I don't remember guests coming in to visit her. She would groan miserably at night from the pain, much like the people yelling down the hall at all times of the day. It was a center for patients at all levels of pain and challenge.

Three weeks into TIRR I was scheduled for bingo games with the nurses and other patients. I could see it was a bright and sunny morning through the wide horizontal window to my left. A nurse had scribbled my activities for the day on a white board, and I recall watching her from my twin-size bed and thinking that these people needed to give me a break. In reality my duties were as simple as waking up, eating, and doing physical therapy, and usually afterwards I would pass out, as my brain had to continuously reconnect my broken pathways.

Bingo was to be held in a separate room, down the hall. I didn't want to go and told Jeri. Thankfully she understood me, but Mom had a different idea. She wanted us to follow the doctor's orders and made my friend wheel me to bingo. A nurse told Jeri to wait outside, as no family or friends were allowed in the games. It was only the nurses with patients. I stared at Jeri as she quickly walked toward the door. She waved goodbye while shrugging her shoulders and looked at me with hopelessness in her eyes, in disbelief that she had to leave. She had known I had wanted her to stay. I had thought she would maybe be able to convince the nurses that I didn't need to be there.

I joined the group of several other patients. We sat around two joined rectangular tables. Everyone seemed a little behind. They talked at kindergarten level. Things were not matching up.

Why am I here? I thought.

I had yet to comprehend the severity of my state.

There was a man across from me having a hard time finding an image of the sunshine on his bingo card. The nurse had just called out in a bright voice, "And who has the sunshine?"

Okay this was bad. The man with the sunshine card was my age, but for some reason he was acting like a five-year-old. What was going on? Mom said I was in a bad accident. I squinted around the room. I must've been way worse than I thought.

"Who has blue socks on their bingo card?" The nurse slowly enunciated each word as she kept flipping her long blonde hair to the side.

Another guy across from me was getting very excited. He just realized he had the blue sock picture on his card.

There was no background music. The room was cold and stale. Sterile. It was silent except for the voice of either the nurse or her assistant. They must have set the bingo cards on the tables before we entered. One patient started laughing, a few were super excited, and a couple were really quiet.

I was one of the really quiet ones.

The physical therapist would wheel me from the third floor to the gym on the first floor. We'd do the recumbent bike for fifteen to twenty minutes while she cheered me on. As I pedaled the bike, I would be frustrated that she couldn't see I was in better shape than to only allow me to exercise on the recumbent bike for such a short amount of time. I wanted to do so much more, or so I had thought. In all reality, I was on a strict brain-injury protocol from the doctors and physical therapists. I still had not emphasized to the physical therapist that I had been training for a marathon; I figured Raul or one of my family members had told her this fact. I don't think they did, and I don't think it would have mattered, as things were different now. I would continue to pedal as I pursed my lips.

I was in the hospital bed on the date of the DC Marine Corp Marathon, the race I was training for when I got hit by a car. I felt stoic. I felt somber. I felt ambushed by circumstance. I felt the tears well up in my eyes before they coursed down my face. No one was bringing up the race. My eyes closed and my body felt numb. *I hate this and this plain out sucks*, I thought. Either my family and friends had forgotten about my race, or they were just happy that I was alive. Now I was running my own marathon of life.

That October, I was lying in bed watching the news about the DC sniper—ten or so people had lost their lives, and there was a huge community of fear in the city where I'd been slated to run my marathon. Children were not left out of the scare, and schools were on alert, using extra safety measures. It was not a good scenario. I felt as if I had entered the twilight zone. What has happened to our world? People are crazy.

I was dozing off to sleep; I was holding Raul's hand. He leaned down and gave me a goodnight kiss on my forehead, like he always did back home before leaving for work.

Today, when I search for my name as a registered runner in the 2002 Marine Corps Marathon, an error webpage appears with the statement: We're sorry, there are no results for Kristin Abello in the 2002 marathon results.

I never showed up to the race.

Martha continued to bring Jacob to the hospital every after-noon—when Raul was ready to see him. In the beginning it was tough for Raul to handle both his toddler son and comatose wife, so his sister did the caretaking. Martha would take Jacob every day to the nearby park to play with his cousins. Of course, when Raul was finally able to see Jacob, it was a very emotional scene for everybody. Jacob clung to Raul and never let go.

It was a tender scene. Even though this does not necessar-ily correlate, seeing Jacob with Raul reminded me of the love I shared with my husband—our bond, our early days. I particularly remember dancing cheek to cheek in the parking lot to Dido when we were still dating. He had pulled his truck over on West Gray Street and turned up the volume. He led me out of his forest-green bronco. It was such a cool truck.

It was a Saturday night out, with the weather an average sixty-five degrees. The evening stars shone over our shoulders. His lips felt so soft as he kissed me. Raul, the sweetheart that he was, had just given me beautiful earrings from his work trip to Mexico. I was elated to know he'd been thinking of me. The lyrics of the song came to me: "I can't breathe / Until you're resting here with me … I don't want to call my friends / They might wake me from this dream."

As we danced in the parking lot holding one another. The only thing between us was the night air. I thought, *I'm falling in love with this wonderful man.*

I missed times with my husband and son.

I missed the family we used to be.

One day I was lying on my hospital bed as Dr. Francisco came into the room with an exuberant smile. He was holding my files as he leaned against the doorway. He looked into the files, then up at me. Staring at him grimly, I thought, *What on earth is he about to say?*

He looked into the files again, studying my medical records from CAT scans to MRIs.

Then he turned to me, looked directly at me, and said, "You don't match your records." He said it with a chuckle, "You don't match your records."

Yes! I probably smiled big. He understood me and how badly I wanted to go home. Finally, someone understands me. I was elated with the simple act of someone, my neurologist, understanding me.

Dr. Francisco said, "You can go home next week, on October 31st."

Excitement washed over me. To go home had been a dream of mine. To be with my boys and sleep in my own bed. The smell of my baby's skin as I cuddled with him on our denim couch in the family room. My prayers and wishes had been granted! I grew even more confident with the existing therapy protocols and worked harder. It made me see how a patient's confidence could improve along with their doctor's faith and confidence in them.

Within the days leading up to my discharge, a number of tests were performed to ensure that I was in a mental and bodily state suitable enough for clearance. My physical therapist, Keri, would wheel me to the back of the rehab room, where everything was fixed up to look like a bedroom in your home. I was looking at the floral green bedsheets as she asked me to get up from my chair, lay on the bed, and then get back up.

After I convinced Keri of my ability to get in and out of bed unaided, she passed me with flying colors and wheeled me out of the rehab room for my next challenge, which was to get in and out of the car. She wheeled me along the hallway in the black wheelchair I had come to love. I was relieved and exhilarated to be outside again. I felt free. I could now see the light at the end of the tunnel. I bit my lip and took a deep inhale as I climbed in and out of our Toyota Sequoia with Keri's and Raul's help. It was a not a straight-arrow, jump-in-and-out-of-car maneuver. I hobbled, left foot up then right foot up, as Keri held me with her hand, under my shoulder. A lot of balance issues came into play, but I did it.

On October 31, 2002, I was going home. I was wheeled out of the car wearing an eye patch the doctors said would help with my double vision and dizziness from looking at things with both eyes. I would wear that patch for a year.

Part 3

Survival

Every end is a beginning.
—Ralph Waldo Emerson

8

A Different Place

I was home in a wheelchair and unable to do almost anything. We became fast friends, the wheelchair and me. I was unable to drive. I needed assistance in the shower, with meals, with getting dressed, and with fixing my hair. I needed assistance going anywhere at all. This was to be my future for the next seven months. The proverb "Patience is a virtue" would be the best quote to describe those times.

My Mom and Poli had to move in with me. I needed all the help I could get. As my "roommates," they cooked for me, took care of me, and did everything for Jacob. Neighbors and support groups from St. Laurence Catholic School brought over food all the time. Even my favorite neighborhood chef, Tommi Gaye Dawson, smiling ear to ear and radiating love, would arrive at my doorstep with my favorite chicken dish and favorite salad with the most scrumptious vinaigrette dressing. The outpouring love I felt during this time was unimaginable. Honestly, I do not recall having to cook for the most part of the first year. Jacob would eat anything we ate, and we had plenty of it. If I had to guess, my first act of cooking was making spaghetti with butter sauce! Family, friends, and neighbors were always taking care of me. The influx of support was overwhelmingly generous. This is the key part to a successful rehab in any situation—the support system. To have a place to fall back into and to have someone always there to catch you. Please find a support system for the patient and you, this is the best gift you can give yourself and an injured loved one. Someone to coach and guide you through these times of unknowns.

After a month of help from every quarter, Ophelia entered the picture. She was a gregarious angel of about five foot three and had been the prior caretaker of Raul's grandmother in Florida. A caring and compassionate caregiver, she lived with me during the day and spent the night at my parents-in-law's. She was the greatest caregiver ever, and I adore her to this day. The aroma of her Cuban cooking always filled our home, she loved to clean with Fabuloso, and she drove me on errands for roughly four months, as well as helped to care for Jacob when he was not with Raul's Mom or Sister. Ofi was such a blessing in such a traumatic time. Ophelia took over from Mom and Pauline, which gave them a break, until eventually they returned to their regular lives in Saudi Arabia and Chicago.

Ophelia, or Ofi as I called her, didn't speak English. And I didn't speak Spanish. It led to a lot of hilarious miscommunications around the house or got us stumped whenever we were in public and tried to achieve common goals. Occasionally, while she drove me, I'd try to point out the next turn in the street, and she'd think I was trying to say "left" in Spanish instead of "right," or right instead of left. As soon as she made the turn, I'd immediately cry out in my slurred voice, "We're going the wrong way!"

Ofi, still driving, would make a gentle motion with her fingers to calm me: "Tranquila, Kristin. Tranquila…" I wouldn't be driving for seven months, and this hilarious episode was one of many.

She also loved to sing Celia Cruz songs to entertain Jacob. She twisted her waist and hips as she sang, "Azuca! Azuca!" in imitation of the Cuban singer. She puckered her lips and mimicked a diva face.

Jacob would watch wide-eyed and try to wiggle his small body like Ofi. When she yelled, "Azzuuuca," he would die laughing, crouched over as if it was the funniest thing he'd ever heard. Actually, they both would die laughing, bent over their knees and cracking up. Ofi was no less than fifty years old at the time, while my little Jacob was just two. It was a sight to see them.

Ofi called Jacob "Yaco" in her deep Spanish accent. "Yaco!"

One day I sat on a ledge in the garage and watched them from a distance. They were patiently waiting for a passing lizard in the front yard. It was a sunny winter day, and the trees were still bare of leaves. Raul's blue RAM truck was parked in the driveway. They finally spotted a lizard, and Jacob grabbed it and held it up by the belly for Ofi to tie a string around the poor lizard's neck, as if it were a collar and they were trying to make a pet dog out of it. Afterwards, Ofi stood by saying encouraging things in Spanish while Jacob walked the lizard!

Jacob ended up being bilingual when she left. When the time came that Ofi's excellent help was no longer needed, I knew he would miss her badly. Ofi returned to Miami. My parents-in-law, Maky and Carlos, still talk to her today, and Ofi still asks about Jacob, her little partner in play. Oh, how she is missed here in Houston.

I noticed in mid-December and January of the new year that things had changed for me. I wanted and needed so much to be normal. I wanted to rush the healing process, but that wasn't happening. I wanted a magic eraser to wipe away all that had happened with the accident and return me to the athletic, young, energetic mom that I had once been.

As I sit and write this, I hold Jacob's second birthday party pictures in my hand. We threw a party for him in December, after I returned from the hospital in October. It was a cowboy-themed party, with about forty children surrounded with every type of farm animal. I want to sob for the person I was at that moment in time—hiding a heavy heart behind a smile. Thankful to God that he kept me on Earth to continue learning and being a teacher for many. My short brunette hair with a few highlights, my face untouched and showing only joy. All of Jacob's friends and class-mates from the St. Laurence Weekday Children's program, Jacob's cousins, my friends from Texas Children's Hospital, and neigh-borhood friends were there.

I kept smiling and leaning down to Jacob's grinning face. He wore his red V-neck sweater and blue long-sleeve Polo under-neath. He was so darn cute and still is a very handsome young man. We sat on the benches that my sister-in-law, Martha, and other moms had decorated with cowboy articles. We ate pizza and sang birthday songs over a pony cake trimmed with light-brown and white borders. The pony had dark-brown hooves, with dark-brown hair—every bodily detail was coated with dark-brown frosting. There was even a red bandana around his neck. Written on the cake was a big red number "2" with "Happy 2nd Birthday Jacob" etched on the surrounding board box. Honestly, I can say today, in all my years of motherhood, it was the best child's birthday cake that I have ever seen.

Today, years later, I had to place a quick call to Martha to recall the name of the birthday venue. Martha, who has an amazing memory, was quick to reply, "Ms. Agnes Café." Lights lit up in my head. Yes, that was the name of the place!

The party attendees took turns riding the horses at the farm. Even Jacob and his dad rode slowly on a trotting horse as I watched from a distance. *Good. My son is enjoying every minute,* I thought. That was all I wanted. I didn't want him to notice anything was different. In reality, did he subconsciously remember this traumatic experience in his little mind? My guess is, yes.

Flipping through Jacob's pictures brings back another memory of that winter. If memory fails us, pictures always tell a story. This one was Raul's Christmas work party. I recall trying not to hobble in my low heels as I walked arm in arm with Raul. He looked so handsome in his coat and tie while I was in a red silk dress and Jimmy Choo strappy sandals. Raul and I interlocked arms—we still do so to this day to help with my balance. Any situation that involves walking, including going down the stairs, remains a challenge. It's sort of an unspoken understanding that Raul and I share; we both know I always need help.

"Hold on, I got it. I got it," I would say to him sometimes. The evening of our first Christmas party (three months after the accident), at Masraff's Restaurant, he lifted me into the passenger seat of the car, and I let him. I needed every ounce of assistance. At the restaurant, everyone said their polite hellos and glad-you're-here type of greetings. At the bar, bottles of vodka, rum, tequila, bourbon, and especially my favorite cabernet wine were staring at me, but I knew I couldn't have any, and I actually didn't want any. I had to sit and rest, as I had used up my energies during the greetings.

Laughter and chattering got louder in the room. Anyone who came to talk with me was very nice and polite. I sipped my ice-water as drinks were passed around. It was almost as if they were making sure they didn't say anything wrong, keeping the conversation simple and light.

I came to the conclusion that after catastrophic life events, people don't know what to say or how to act. In all reality, we just want them to be real, to say what is on their mind. Acting as if something never happened is not the way to go. The elephant in the room scenario is not the way to go. It is truly okay to tell the survivor you are happy they are here and alive. That will mean the world to them.

Raul and I had to excuse ourselves early from our first evening out. We were going home, and not too soon because I couldn't socialize anymore. My mind and body were shutting down. It was just enough stimulation for me to take. I had wanted to stay, but I knew my new normal was to say my goodbyes early in the evening—to take care of me. This was the beginning of my journey to life-long self-awareness; noticing things were very different, not the way they use to be. Being self-aware is a must in every person's life, especially during recovery of anything, from TBI to any health debilitating issue.

In spite of situations like this, I never seemed to lose hope. I set internal goals for myself, making sure to never miss a session of physical therapy or skip any at-home exercises that were assigned to me. Reading inspirational readings and having faith always kept me going toward the finish line of rehab, today and ultimately forever. I would tie a green resistance band to the back porch doorknob. I would continue to do the prescribed exercises at home. Primarily they were arm rehab exercises. I knew how important it was to do them, as I expected my patients at the hospital to do what I asked of them at home. I would always get after them to practice at home what we did at the hospital. Now, I was the patient.

Maky always took me to physical therapy come rain or shine. Physical therapy at TIRR came bundled in a larger after-care program called "The Challenge Program." With this, patients would take cooking classes, do physical therapy, and participate in group roundtable discussions. The room was always cold, and I remember all the mentors and therapists being very supportive and wanting to help each patient individually. During discussions, no one could have a decent conversation, as we were all in different phases of recovery. One thing we had in common was that we had been patients at TIRR. We had to speak in turns about what had happened to us. What kind of truth could my body tell? What could anyone's body around the roundtable tell? Imagine if I could say exactly what my body had been through that September day. I have to suspect that God protects us during hurt, and I had forgotten everything that took place that morning of the car accident. As we all shared our stories around the room, it became clear that most patients were motorcycle-accident victims. I was the only one involved in a pedestrian-vehicle accident. I remember being observant and looking around while comparing myself. One man kept laughing uncontrollably. Everyone seemed out of it—almost as if they were drunk or on drugs.

But we all talked in a slurred voice, including me. *Shit, this is bad.* I would inhale deeply. *This is the new normal for me and I have got to get better,* I would think to myself.

TIRR was now too far from where I lived on the outskirts of Houston. The thirty-to-forty-five-minute drive as a passenger would make me dizzy and nauseous. With the doctors' permission, I opted for the outpatient therapy program at the former Polly Ryon Memorial Hospital in Richmond, which was closer to where I lived. Maky would take me on the twenty-minute drive to Polly Ryon on the freeway headed southwest. We continued this routine, four times a week, for months on end.

Judith, Charlotte, and Craig were my therapists when I arrived at Polly Ryon. When I was first evaluated, my right arm completely failed the test, my balance was off, and my vision was impaired. The first time I went on the balance beam to practice walking, I tried balancing on my own, but no luck, I simply fell off the beam (it was only maybe a foot off the floor). Judith then wrapped a chest strap around my torso and walked alongside to guide and hold me. A few months later I could walk without the strap, unaided. This took a lot of mental readiness within myself. *The harder I work, the less I will have to come here*, I would think to myself. Mind over matter, I have to move forward for Jacob, for Raul…for Me.

Finally, by June, I had worked myself into graduating from the physical therapy program.

I was due for a follow-up visit with Dr. Francisco one morning. I was with Raul and hoping for good news. I was wearing my workout clothes as I entered the cold and low-lit hospital room at TIRR. It felt good to be seeing the doctor who had taken such good care of me, but also it felt good because my in-patient days were over.

The waiting room looked like something out of an episode of *Grey's Anatomy.*

As busy doctors walked by the room and from hall to hall, Dr. Francisco happily approached us in one of the dimly lit doctors' offices and asked his pertinent brain-injury checkup questions. After about ten minutes of questioning, he proceeded to give me the big news.

"Congratulations," he said. "You're released from TIRR Hospital Neurology Outpatient. You don't need to see me again."

I said, "That's it?"

"That's it," he said.

I was saying goodbye to the doctor and the people who had helped save my life. It was bittersweet—saying goodbye to hospital life and hello to the new life that awaited me. Breaking unknown barriers was to be the future that God gifted me. Internally I was scared, I knew I still had lots of hurdles to overcome. I was going to keep moving forward, though.

It had been so long since I enjoyed a glass of wine, and I felt it was appropriate to ask if I could have one.

"Can I now have a glass of wine?" I asked slowly with my eyes squinting and my eyebrows lifted with hope.

"No," he said. "Maybe a sip."

"What?" I asked.

"Okay," he replied. "One glass, and that's it."

"Thank you," I said. I wanted to celebrate!

Raul and I celebrated my discharge from TIRR at our favorite breakfast restaurant, Buffalo Grill, with an order of their most delicious and buttery pancakes. They were the very ones I was dreaming of on the morning of the accident. The melted butter and hot syrup drizzled perfectly on the cakes, making every bite to die for.

That July of 2003 I ran a half-marathon in San Francisco. The Chronicle Marathon was one of the many goals I had set for myself and placed at my bedroom door as a daily reminder.

During the race, I ran and walked some of the distance. Views of the Golden Gate Bridge and Alcatraz reminded me of

the past. I was back here again, doing a race to demonstrate my
new beginning and re-entry to life.

I eventually wrote a note to Dr. Francisco, expressing
my excitement at completing the half-marathon, ten months
post-accident.

I didn't tell Dr. Francisco, though, of the fight against the
double vision as I ran. Everything before me was twofold. It was
screwy, complete chaos. There was a shifting, sketchy mirage of
many trees dancing together, splitting and overlapping. One stop
sign appeared split; the sidewalk was broken into two images that
kept crisscrossing like scissor blades. I saw people interlacing and
entwining like an artist's splattered oil paintwork—people with
four legs, four eyes, even four arms. I'd never been on drugs before, but this must be what it felt like to have those psychedelic
acid trips or hallucinogenic mushrooms.

I had to stop, then put my hands on my knees. I looked down.
"Uncle, I can't see. I keep seeing double. I just can't continue,"
I said.

Uncle Alen was running, catching up to me. "Kristin, cover
one eye," he shouted in his deep voice, holding up one palm to
his eye. "It will make it much better!"

I did, and sure enough I could see clearly for a time. Because
I also had some cognition issues, I hadn't thought of that simple
task of bringing my old patch to the race. I didn't forget, I just
hadn't thought ahead that I would experience turbulence during
my run or walk up the hills in San Francisco.

Friends from Houston and big brother Sy had come to support me. After an emotional cheer at the finish line, we celebrated at a nearby breakfast café. I had so wished my husband was with me to share this turning point, but Jacob had fallen sick last minute with the croup—the whooping cough that sounds like a seal. Raul didn't want me to miss the race I had worked so hard toward. So, I went, and he took care of Jacob.

My double vision was surgically corrected one year post accident. Both of my parents had arrived for the procedure as well as Raul's parents. Something I have stated throughout the book is that having a support group, whether it be a friend, family, or any support group, is the number one priority to a successful future for any traumatic injury victim or for anything that life throws your way. I remember that Jacob was to play soccer when I had the surgery, and the next day I made sure to be at Jacob's game.

In order to surgically fix my eye problem, ophthalmologist Dr. Kathryn Musgrove said I would not be able to look up (be an astronaut) or look all the way down (be a pilot) without seeing double. Check and check, I did not want to be either. She was right. Today, years later, looking either way down or up is an invitation to more double vision. For this reason, I can't play tennis. However, the worst—the double vision looking forward—was removed. To this day, I automatically close one eye when looking up or down. Make sure to have your doctor recommend the best eye specialist if you are battling with any ocular issues.

Something totally unexpected was still ahead of me. I went to visit my friend Heather Gunn in Lubbock, Texas after I left the hospital. I had met Heather the first year I moved to the United States in 1985. In school, she had a locker beneath mine, and one day I was sitting by myself at lunch when Heather reached over and asked me something. I don't remember what it was, but she was very friendly and nice. Everything was new to me, as I'd just moved from Saudi Arabia. I thought, *I want to be friends with this girl because she's nice to me. Nobody else is talking to me.*

Eventually I had more friends in junior high. However, with Heather, and later Erica, we all remained tight, like sisters. We argued, but then we'd be fine two minutes later. Heather's mom couldn't believe that was possible in the midst of all our never-ending girl drama.

Heather's home on Highland Knolls Drive was my second home. Later, after college, Heather and her high school sweetheart married and moved to Lubbock. I still kept up my visits and when I came to see her post accident, I was in recovery mode and wasn't driving yet. But I was no longer in a wheelchair and my speech had improved.

We were both young moms in our twenties, and I was excited to meet my best friend's first baby. She had gone through challenges during childbirth, and due to my brain injury, I didn't have a good picture of what had taken place.

It was a wonderful opportunity to catch up.

Over the last months, I had gained weight, and I drank water all day. I was unbelievably thirsty all the time. The weight thing, who knows. My guess is that since my body underwent such a trauma it was acclimating to my new internal normal. I certainly was not as active (as in my prior days in my early twenties) and always had a big appetite. A good fifteen pounds was gained, and on a short person that is a lot! At Heather's place I just drank and drank. There were empty water bottles all over her house. My thirst was unquenchable.

Her husband, Brandon, was in medical school at the time. He saw all the empty water bottles and said to Heather, "I think Kristin might have something called diabetes insipidus."

Heather told me what Brandon said.

I made an appointment with an endocrinologist the following week.

It was confirmed. I did have diabetes insipidus. It turned out that my pituitary gland was affected by the accident. I was prescribed a nose spray that halted my extreme thirst.

As I've continued to heal from my brain injury, my pituitary gland has gradually improved back to normal. Sometimes, though, when I become very thirsty, I can't help but think my diabetes insipidus is coming back. During such moments, my mouth will feel as though it's stuffed with cotton balls. This must be a natural fear, I say to myself.

Please be sure to have your neurologist recommend the best endocrinologist, or any other relevant specialists, to check for secondary ailments, as there are many hidden illnesses that sometimes go unnoticed with a brain injury.

I also struggled with staying awake since I needed as much as nine hours of daily sleep. Regular naps, according to the doctors, were a part of recovery, as my brain was still rewiring itself.

One day while I was at an appointment with the endocrinologist for my diabetes insipidus, another doctor was also present. By this time, I was in my late twenties and had been discharged from all rehabilitation. I was very ready to have more babies. Before the accident, I had wanted a sizable family; but now I just wanted a sibling for Jacob—at least one.

I asked the doctor if he thought another pregnancy would be safe for me. He repeated what previous doctors had told me: "Do not get pregnant. You've had a traumatic brain injury. Your body is still recovering."

My strong desire for another child would not go away. I ended up seeing a high-risk pregnancy doctor. As I sat on the exam table, he asked me questions about my health, my recovery, and raising Jacob. Once I answered them, he looked over my file, then back at me. "I don't see any reason why you can't get pregnant," he said.

"The high risk pregnancy doctor said that I can get pregnant!" I exclaimed to Raul when I got home.

Another doctor from that clinic later prescribed some fertility medicine.

After about three or four months, I ended up getting pregnant with Colin. It was the polar opposite of my first pregnancy with Jacob, when I was in my mid-twenties, young, healthy, and athletic. During and after my second pregnancy, I finally understood everyone's concerns, and why I was told not to get pregnant.

I was dramatically sick. I vomited several times a day for nine months and gained around fifteen or twenty pounds—not nearly enough. I was prescribed Zofran for my never-ending sickness. It was an anti-nausea medication commonly prescribed for cancer patients.

I still vomited daily, however. I recall a scene I made while at the vegetable section of the grocery store not far from home. I had entered for a quick food run. As I started choosing oranges, I felt it coming up my throat. I made for the bathroom but couldn't get there fast enough, and I started heaving my breakfast tacos all over the floor.

A kind grocery staffer ran to get a broom or mop and stood cleaning up my vomit as I covered my mouth in embarrassment, apologizing. I began to live in perpetual fear of my vomiting sprees. In addition to diabetes insipidus, the vomiting episodes haunted me until bedrest at thirty weeks.

With such constant sickness, I was sure Colin was going to be a girl.

Her name will be Gabriella, I thought.

Later, when the ultrasound showed the baby in me was a boy, I was convinced the nurses didn't know what they were talking about. His privates must have been hiding behind another organ. With time, Raul and I began deciding on a name for the coming baby boy. We wholeheartedly agreed that his first or middle name would be Andrew after our beloved Father Drew, who was my first memory as I came out of coma—my second chance at life.

Raul and I were watching *The Amazing Race* at our newly built Greatwood home when we finally arrived at a name for our second child. *The Amazing Race* was a reality series in which teams competed in a race around the world. We were particularly inspired by one of the contestants named Colin. He was a brave and gutsy competitor and turned out to be the winner for that season. We had hit on a name for our son—Colin Andrew. Perfect match.

Raul and I love watching *The Amazing Race* to this day.

Come July 15, 2004, our fourth wedding anniversary, I went to see my OB-GYN for my weekly checkup. He retained me because I had gone into labor. I lay on the bed with Raul by my side, while the OB-GYN sat in a nearby chair with hand on chin, thinking and gazing at the white tile floor. Finally, he stood up. "We're taking the baby. We're taking the baby at 5:30 p.m."

I was admitted to Texas Women's Hospital, and Colin arrived in the world at thirty-seven weeks on the dot, weighing in at seven pounds, fifteen ounces. He was a good size for being early. Colin was the most laid-back baby in the world. He arrived three and a half years after Jacob, which was a little over two years after the accident. Call it a coincidence or synchronicity that our second son was born on our anniversary.

I had dreamed of having three kids before thirty-five, and now, with the medical recommendations to not get pregnant again, I had to stop at two. We all wish and pray for wonderful things in our future, and I came to realize God had different plans for me.

Five years soon passed after the traumatic brain injury. I had been on autopilot ever since the accident that almost took my life. "Touch and go" as Raul always explains it. I became grateful for simple everyday things, like Colin sucking on his orange pacifier with the green knob up under his nose. He was cute as a little nugget, especially with that extra baby fat at age two. He always held on to his stuffed blue puppy with a tight grip. Puppy went with him everywhere, especially to sleep.

I recall he had that puppy with him when we went to see my grandmother, who at the later stages of her life was placed on bed rest. We wanted to bring the boys to their cultural roots and give them an experience of their Armenian heritage.

My paternal grandmother, Kristin Saleri, who we called Kristinmama, was a renowned, legendary visual artist in Turkey. She was partially blind during Colin's early years, but this did not stop my grandmother's grit and grace. She was painting until her last days.

Colin would stare as he sucked on his pacifier, mesmerized at his brother, Jacob, hugging Kristinmama. We were all seated next to her bed in her private room. Grandma's caretaker would move pillows and make her more comfortable on the couch. It was a plain little white room, meant for just a brief stay. Surviving the genocide and surviving the car crash were connected journeys of our will to survive. We were here today holding hands on the couch and that's all that mattered. To share the gift of life with family and friends in the union of Sy and Selin's marriage. We had all arrived for Sy and Selin's wedding at a small chapel, The Holy Cross Armenian Church, built in 1681. Jacob and Colin both joined us as we sat on the first row of the church. We were all staring with intense amazement the next hour watching The Armenian Orthodox Priest wearing his Byzantine mitre.

Later we proceeded to the reception. We had decided to leave Colin with a Turkish babysitter who did not speak English and prayed for the best. We thought that this was better for him, as we didn't want him getting restless at the reception.

We arrived downstairs at the outdoor patio at the breathtaking Feriye Palace, overlooking the Bosphorus Sea. The famous Bosphorus Bridge in the Taksim District was a gorgeous backdrop as we all danced the night away.

Grandma had wanted to live long enough to see Sy married to an Armenian woman, and this was a dream come true for her. I remember her being wheeled to the wedding in a glamorous dress where she remained watching the ceremony from behind a table. She passed about a month after the wedding.

I was also grateful for my children's general development. Jacob and Colin had their elementary years at St. Laurence Catholic School in Sugar Land and St. Cecilia Catholic School in Houston. I was always sure to be involved in parent activities, from helping as a room mom for their specific grade, taking candid portraits for the students, or helping with the school auction.

Colin was quite the crier in his younger years, and there was a time I had to peel him off the car at a school drop off. Soon I got worried—something had to change, since my fourth grader would not get out of the car. Raul and I took a leap of faith and had him enrolled at a private, all-boys, liberal arts school down the road, Western Academy. The campus looked like the set of the TV show *Little House on the Prairie*. In my mind, this seemed like a perfect fit. Plenty of outside space to run around in. It resembled Burgaz Island, the Princess Island in Istanbul, where we would spend endless summers at Kristinmama's house.

On the first day, Colin still refused to leave the car. He locked the doors and hunkered down in the back seat. Mr. Jason Hebert, the headmaster, who was there to walk Colin out of the car, for a quick moment could do nothing to convince Colin to come out.

All three adults—Raul, me, and Mr. Hebert—were weary. We sat in the outdoor garden located among oak trees and rich greenery. The school's classrooms were housed in little cottage-looking houses from where we sat. With his arms thrown over the bench, the headmaster shook his head and said seriously, "If only he would give all that energy to something positive, he could change the world."

I took those words to heart and repeated them to Colin. Within a short time, he was able to exit the car on his own in the mornings and proceed toward the open doors of his new school.

My son's courage made me look at my own life afresh.

9

Reflections

He rode his big wheel, wearing a blue-and-white short-sleeve shirt. He had shaggy, dirty-blonde hair. I was watching with love because I'd always wanted a big wheel. Joshua rode up and down the alleyway between two apartment complexes. His mother opened the window a few times and shouted from the second story, "Be careful. Get off the street!"

As I watched intently, a four-door station wagon turned the corner into the alleyway. I saw it coming down the street and next thing I knew, in the blink of an eye, the wagon was running him over. It made such a loud screeching sound. I was aged four and still remember the incident as if it happened yesterday—the horrifying image is forever tattooed in my memory.

Having witnessed that as a young, innocent child, was God preparing me for something similar in my future? Was the similarity in street names—Banbury and Sansbury—a coincidence? Synchronicity? Or am I reading too much into it? I never learned whether Joshua was okay.

This was California in the seventies. It was the time when personal freedom, love, and rock 'n' roll was an everyday vibe. I remember the strawberry fields across the street, and my brother and I always playing outside in the alley and going to the pool.

It's possible that the very spirit of the seventies rubbed off on me and can be said to have contributed to my love for Sy's city, San Francisco. Apart from San Francisco serving as the place where I ran my first big race, it was the city of adorable hippies in defiance of social expectations. I visited my brother more times than I could count, content to spend time with his circle of friends and Pauline, my ever-ready companion for good times and shopping.

One day Pauline and I were having fun shopping the streets of San Francisco. We were staying at some boutique hotel near Sy's home in Upper Haight. We decided to idle away on the streets before having dinner with Sy's friends in the evening. A brown-haired lady came up to us as we walked in Union Square, offering to read our palms. I have already told the story of the psychic and of how her reaction to whatever she read in my palm terrified me.

I had the accident one month later. I still wonder to this day how the story might have been different if I'd gone to the church to pray with her as she had suggested. I often ponder over the life the psychic must be living now with such a genuine gift of foretelling. One thing is for certain, I will never forget her look of desperation—wanting me to go with her to the nearby church and pray with her. What did she foresee? Could it have been Father Drew or any of the priests visiting me in the hospital and anointing my head with holy oil as my cold body lay in a grim coma?

Would the psychic remember me if she saw me today?

I swear I saw her look-alike on a bike ride with my sister-in-law, April, in Avon, Colorado the other day. But it couldn't be her, since this lady looked to be in her twenties, eighteen years younger than the psychic would look right now.

Bad things unfortunately come without invitation. The accident was intense for everybody, not only me. It was like walking on eggshells; traveling on the battlefield of TBI was unknown to both family and friends. There was no book, no video, no "how-to" guide on making life easier for TBI patients, family, friends, and caretakers. Of course, no one would interfere with the work of the doctors, as everyone wanted to say and do the right thing.

From my father's point of view, there were gaps in communication with patient management and different levels of sensitivity to the family's anguish. This is something he still alludes to even today because he wasn't very happy with the glitches in updates, especially during the first seven days. Specifically, my Dad had questions about whether and when I was going to come out of the coma. Once I survived the first forty-eight hours, that question became more persistent. The family wasn't getting any satisfactory answers. It became a point of friction, especially between him and his twin brother, Uncle Alen, who was a medical doctor and psychiatrist from Washington, DC.

Eventually, Raul and Dad were told on the third day that if I remained in coma for more than seven days the damage to my brain would be exponentially bigger. Every day after the seventh day posed further danger to my later quality of life. The first seventy-two hours were extremely difficult emotionally. Raul and my parents took turns sleeping on the floor in the visitation area of the intensive care unit of Memorial Hermann because they wanted to provide me with twenty-four-hour coverage. The hospital had special visiting hours, but they were there for me, twenty-four hours a day.

Dad would say without any hesitation that he personally learned more about life during that first week, during those long hours at intensive care, than at any other period of his life. He saw the best and the worst sides of living. In the early hours of the evening especially, lots of trauma patients were being wheeled in. Many of them were motorcycle-accident victims or people who had fallen from ladders while installing antennas or TV cables.

My family saw dozens of people living what they lived through on that Sunday morning after my accident. People in a state of shock assailed the hospital to see loved ones, some of them far more emotional than my family. Others got reports much sooner than what my loved ones experienced. Some reports weren't good—my family would see priests arrive to provide last blessings, and everyone knew what that meant. My father observed all the hugging and crying that went on. When you regularly see such intense moments, he would later tell me, you assign a different value to the meaning of life.

There was a particular incident Dad witnessed one evening. The mother, father, and brother of an accident victim were arguing in the lobby about who stood to inherit what if the victim didn't wake from his coma. On another day, Dad was approached by a chaplain who offered to enter my room and give me some last blessing rites. Dad told him, "No. Death is not happening for my daughter," and graciously walked away from the chaplain.

Raul tells the story of a trauma victim who shared a unit with me in ICU. The patient was across the hall from me and the curtains were not drawn. He had a hole drilled in his skull to relieve brain pressure. I later learned these were called burr holes. One day the patient sneezed or coughed, and fluid came spraying out of the tube in the top of his head, like a jet. Raul watched as the nurses wiped up the fluid. He was a young person suffering from an infection from pork, or so Raul remembers hearing.

In spite of all these life and death medical stories, there were a few humorous moments. During that first week in ICU, an interesting drama unfolded for Dad. He and Raul had spent the night keeping watch over me. Around eight the next morning, he walked over to the nearby Marriott Hotel in the Memorial Hermann complex, where they had rented several rooms for family members and other relatives who stayed over. He wanted to shower and take a nap before returning in the afternoon.

Mom told him, "When you're coming back, please bring my blouse." She described a maroon blouse in her carry-on luggage in the hotel room.

Dad went to the hotel and took the elevator to the fifth or sixth floor. My parents' room was to the right of the elevator. The door was open, and he noticed two housekeepers working in the room. The young ladies were watching television and not necessarily cleaning. Dad told them, "Ladies, thank you so much. You don't have to finish your cleaning right now. What I would like to do is take a rest. So, if you don't mind, please come back later to clean the room."

They thanked him and left. Dad shut the door.

He remembered to look for Mom's maroon-colored blouse, so he went to look through her carry-on. He couldn't find the blouse. He said to himself, "Well, I'll worry about it later on," since he still had some time.

He entered the bathroom for a shower. Hanging on the door was a red bra, which struck him as a bit unusual because he'd never seen my Mom wear a red bra. He thought, *Well, obviously the accident has affected each of us differently, and this is how she's expressing her anxiety—with color.*

He didn't touch the bra but left it hanging there. When he came out of the shower, he noticed there was also a pair of red underwear in the bathroom. Again, he said to himself, *This is very bizarre. I've never seen my wife with red underwear and a red bra. But, before I fall asleep, I better find this maroon blouse that she asked me to bring her.*

He went through the luggage again, but in a more hurried way, as he was ready to sleep. The more he couldn't find the blouse, the more agitated he became. So, he dumped everything out and then said, "Well, there is no blouse here. Enough already."

He called Mom and said, "Look, I'm going to bed. I cannot find your blouse. Where is it?"

She quietly told him, "No, it's on the very top of the chair."

Here he was, making a mess of the carry-on. Dad said, "Okay, look. Let me see what I can do." He went back again to look. No chair, no blouse, no nothing.

He told Mom, "Listen, I can't find it," and hung up.

Suddenly, it dawned on him that he could be in a different room and the red underwear and bra belonged to somebody else.

He went into a panic. In fact, as the realization set in, he could hear hotel security communicating over walkie-talkies down the hallway. And there he was, totally naked and half wet. Dad thought, *They've realized that there's been a break-in. They're coming in to arrest me, and they're going to say, "Here is this pervert in the room going through somebody's private stuff."* This is going to be quite a story in the local media.

Immediately, he got dressed and called the receptionist. "Ma'am," he said. "I'm Nansen Saleri. Something terrible has happened. I want you to know my daughter is in a coma at Memorial Hermann, and out of my confusion and sleep deprivation, I got into the wrong room and made a mess of it. I'm terribly sorry. Please be aware of this. I'm going to put everything back. It's going to look very disorderly, but here is my name and I will take care of whatever damages there are. But I want to make sure that you understand that this was a most innocent accident."

The lady at the reception desk was understanding. "Sir, don't worry. We'll take care of it. You have nothing to worry about."

Dad wrote a little note of apology to the room guest explaining the situation.

He went back to his "real" room—which, by the way, had been properly cleaned—and took a nap. When he returned with the blouse to the hospital, he told the family the story. It was the first time they had laughed since my accident.

I have no doubt the hands of God were on this scene, lightening up the situation through humor.

Dad says today that he thinks the most important thing he rediscovered was the love and loyalty of the community. One determines the meaning of love and true loyalty in the darkest hours. My family knew infinite love from everywhere in the world: from family and friends in Istanbul, Europe, Dhahran, California, Washington, DC and, of course, here in Houston. We felt the support.

My college friends Jeri, April, Jamie, and Keri frequently came to visit. My whole high school group got to know about the accident. Childhood friend Heather Gunn's father came to the hospital, as Heather was on bed rest from childbirth and lived far away.

Heather Mahan, along with other friends, had bought tickets for the Dixie Chicks concert in Dallas before the accident, and I'd agreed to go. On the day of the event, which was days after the accident, I didn't show up and she couldn't reach me. Thinking I had changed my mind or was busy with motherhood, the group of friends went to the Blue Goose restaurant and later had a nice time at the concert.

When Heather later found out about my accident, it was through an email from our mutual friend Keely. Heather was sitting in her office in Dallas. Her heart fell hard. She was still taking care of a relative who'd just had a heart transplant, so she couldn't come to see me immediately. She says today that it killed her emotionally, but Raul and my Dad talked with her. She still felt helpless.

Eventually she visited from Dallas after I left TIRR. We had a spa day and, later, some dinner with other high school friends.

I soon pushed the traumatic accident to the back of my mind—or at least I minimized it. I was happy to be alive. I knew my purpose was to help others that have been through any kind of trauma. Actually, this was always my purpose, but now even more so. It was engraved in me. It was a direct hit from God. I was in therapy shortly afterwards to gradually stabilize, but not to dig deep into the emotional hurt it may have caused. It was never talked about among family. It was never brought up by the therapist either, or if it was, I don't remember. I recall focusing on our next family vacation for sixteen people. I remember asking the therapist how I was going to handle talking with so many people. Although I loved each one of my in-laws dearly, the numbers were too much for a post-brain-injury patient to process. I needed quiet time and should have made this a priority for myself. I was

relearning the new me and mourning the loss of the old me. If
you are a friend, family member, or caretaker of a trauma patient,
please give yourself grace for the new normal. I should have given
myself grace in this department. As I share this with you today,
please know that a TBI survivor needs quiet time. A must. Post-
accident, I have come to be aware of this and do my best to adhere
to my internal needs as a post-traumatic-brain-injury survivor. As
a mom and a wife, we are needed so much on every level. If you
have been afflicted with a TBI, please take time off for *you*.

I shouldn't have minimized such a traumatic experience at
all. But did I know I was doing this at the time? No, I didn't
know. I wanted to be laser-focused in bringing up Jacob and,
later, focused on my second son, Colin. I had no time to reflect
on the accident's aftermath. It was up and go, go, go all the time.
I never skipped a beat. Family or friends would ask how I was,
and I always said, "Good." I was on autopilot.

I didn't know how to say, in the right way, that I needed help.
Actually, in my mind I didn't have time to worry about myself. I
wanted everything to be okay. My faith was in abundance—I was
gifted life, my husband, and two healthy boys. That was enough
to keep me looking forward. Although good direction after brain
injury would have been very helpful. A one-on-one Brain Injury
Coach or a Life Coach would have been perfect.

Reflecting on it now, the accident itself should have been re-
viewed and discussed, when the time was right, with the guidance
of a therapist. What were the appropriate things to say, as well as
the inappropriate, to a survivor of a trauma?

When was the right time? I would say in the first quarter when stability and survival are taking place. From day one, all family, friends, and caretakers should be informed that this is going to be a long journey. Having a therapist to aid family and friends on how to hold hands with the brain injury survivor and how to hold conversations about the situation post injury would have done wonders. A must is to have a therapist and priest (or leader of your belief system) to hold the victim's hands during the process, and their loved ones, too. The truth was that no one knew what to say and would dodge the subject to talk me up instead. There was no space to collectively grieve the pain.

I recall phone calls where people would ask, vaguely, "How are you?" and "I'm so glad you are okay," before going on to talk non-stop about stupid shit I didn't even care about. They must have been nervous talking to me. People don't know how to act or what to say to survivors of any catastrophic accident.

During this time, I could see that people thought I was back to normal. They didn't know any better, since I did my best to present myself that way. It was unintentional, and they meant well. For instance, on one of our big family vacations we were off to Disney World with around fifteen of us; this included seven kid cousins aged seven and under and all of us parents. My accident had happened within the last few years. I was struggling with the residual effects of head trauma but didn't want to accept it. I was always hoping I would snap back to normal.

I asked Raul's brother if I ought to ride the bumper cars. He said, "Yes, why not?" Raul didn't say no either. They wanted me to have fun. The focus was on the little cousins, and rightfully so. In retrospect I should have bowed out from riding the bumper cars. I was sitting in that car among so many little black beetles with the black poles thinking, "This can't be healthy." I knew better than to be riding in a bumper car. I started to go fast, but instead of hitting other cars, I made sure to race away to prevent getting bumped.

When I was bumped the first time, my head got thrashed in so many directions my brain was about to pop out of my skull. When everyone got off, they kept saying they had had so much fun. I couldn't even walk straight. It was the most horrid experience. But I didn't want to miss out on important fun moments with the family. I acted normal. I wanted to be the fun mom for my kids and their cousins. Today, it would be easier for me to back off. I wish I had been wise enough back then.

In short, I needed to be easy on me; give myself grace. If you are still reading this book and are a victim, or a friend or family member of someone who was hurt, please give yourself grace. It is a must. The injury itself is a mountain to climb.

The "noise factor" (or overstimulation) was another point of difficulty. I found it hard, and still do, to be around loud and progressive sounds. This aspect was very, very intense during the first five years of recovery, and lasts to present day. As time passed, it most definitely improved, and now I know how to manage it better; I know what choices to make in order to protect myself. With raising two boys, it was a challenge in the early days; now not as much, as they are older and self-sufficient. If you have little ones, please have family, friends, or hired help around to help you—if you can afford it. The trick is to stay ahead of it and have your days planned with who will be there to help you.

Recently, Raul and I were at a friend's house for a Halloween get-together. I sat enjoying my glass of wine. A lady sitting nearby on an ottoman had flashing lights on her costume headband. It was so fun and cute, but it threw my eyesight for a loop. I entered the twilight zone, praying I would not pay for it later. She was talking away to me. I thought, "How do I tell this nice lady that the lights are bothersome?" I knew she was having fun, and I didn't want to be the bearer of bad news. At the same time, I also knew I would lose a few days, meaning I would need to resort to a quiet room to heal from the flashing and blinking lights.

Finally, I said to her, "You will have to excuse me, but the lights are too bright for me." Of course, I said it as nice as I could.

I walked away to sit across from her, hoping that she would get the message and turn off the blinking lights on her forehead. She continued talking as I moved away. I told the hostess (who had one on as well), "So sorry, it's a brain thing. I hate to be a party pooper, but I can't do the flashing lights."

She immediately turned her lights off and told her friends to do the same. I felt terrible even though I knew she was a friend who knew my story. Similar stories like this one have taken place throughout the years of healing, even today. Basically, you have to be your own best advocate, as no one will go up to bat for you. Everyone has their own worries and concerns with their own lives.

Years ago, we attended a birthday party at Dave and Busters. There, the flashing neon lights and loud music were hard to bear. The arcade machines kept going ding, ding, ding. You walked in and it was like everything was droning and dinging. Every loud noise possible was present. You know what I'm talking about if you've been there. I stayed for about thirty minutes before I realized I couldn't do it. Who knows, I thought I could, but in reality, the piercing noises flooded my brain, and it was like my forehead was being crushed. It was no different from having someone roast pieces of my brain over a fire with marshmallow sticks. My ears were being twisted from the inside in opposite directions. I left to sit in the car out in the empty parking lot. I just wanted to do "normal" things like everyone else and would always try. I simply could not, and I am happy to say today that I can bow out and manage myself accordingly.

Another instance of overstimulation was at a gym where a friend and I occasionally worked out. There were neon-orange lights from ceiling flush mounts, and the music was blaring at full capacity. I was running on the treadmill, working the rowing machine, and doing strength training with free weights. The lights kept flashing from above, and the workout pop music was enough to blast the nerves out of my brain. The glare was too intense for my eyesight. I headed home feeling like viscous liquid slowly swirling down a funnel. I plopped into bed and remained in silence for two days.

More recently, roofers came to work at our house and banged away all day. It set the dogs to barking. Raul came home to briefly check on the roofers and noticed it was "crazy time" for our pets, so he took them to PetSmart for the day.

The banging continued. Raul and I argued about the overpowering noise problem. I wanted him to understand that my brain couldn't handle such strenuous noise. "It's all too much for me to handle," I said to Raul. The look on Raul's face said he thought I was still suffering from carryovers of stimulus related issues from the past.

After Raul left, I retreated to a dark room till the roofers left; this is all I crave when moments of overstimulation happen. My little guy, Colin, fifteen at the time, didn't understand why I was upset or crying. To him we needed a new roof, and the roofers were rightfully doing their job. I tried to explain my bursting nerves to my son, but my brain hurt too much. I felt better when I was in a cool, dark, and quiet room, like the laundry room, where I listened to calming music by Enya.

I finally sent an email to Dr. Francisco (before the pandemic took over our world) telling him of my troubles:

Hi Dr. Francisco,

Hope your 2020 is off to a great start. I have a post-TBI question. I've stayed focused on quiet time, but I get distraught when in the presence of loud noises. Anything else you suggest? It's a brain thing, not a physical thing, as I was able to walk and drive and am fine otherwise. What could this be? Thank you.

Dr. Francisco replied:

Hi Kristin,

I am sorry to hear about this. You are right, the heightened sensitivity to stimuli (including noise and bright lights) is most likely related to the brain injury. Unfortunately, the only way around this is to avoid the stimulus. I am also glad that you are trying to employ relaxation and creating a low-stimulus environment. Desensitization therapy (by a qualified psychologist) may help, but not guaranteed to be effective. Let me know if you want to try this. Wish I could have been of more help.

Comfort filled me up as I read the email from the doctor; it helped walk me back into life, again.

A doctor with positive and personable bedside manners is always a blessing in my book. Lesson learned and shared always: Ask for help no matter the situation. Take away any fear you may be feeling and ask for help. This can only benefit *you*.

10

Surviving Today

November 16, 2019

Dear Driver,

I am asked by the Narrative Spark instructor to write you a letter. Specifically, she wanted us to write something about a traumatic experience from our lives. She noted that some therapists ask their patients to write a letter about a distressing experience they've had. You came to mind.

I've always wondered what you were thinking or not thinking. For the past seventeen years, I have forgiven you and always felt sorry for you for having to live with that inner pressure, knowing you almost killed an innocent human being. A wife. A mother. A daughter. A granddaughter. A friend.

How did it feel hitting a person at 25 mph? Were you truly going 25 mph? Did you battle with nightmares? I can't imagine having to live with that day in and day out. I learned you were at a wine dinner. How late did you stay? Was it too early that Sunday morning for you to be aware of your surroundings on the road? Were you over-served the night before? I have so many questions.

Why didn't you ever apologize? At the least, a simple letter to my husband and parents, who had to live through the nightmare, could have helped.

You were always forgiven in my heart as you were by my family. I do thank you for having held the prayerful vigil for me, as I know every prayer helped keep me alive. God was kind enough to give me a second chance. Everything happens for a reason. I wish you peace, love, and happiness throughout your lifetime. Today, I can say thank you for giving me this gift of opportunity to help other victims of traumatic brain injury or any living trauma at all.

Love,
Kristin Abello

I had chosen to write this letter not long after I read the driver's trial deposition in September of 2019. I don't know why I waited so many years after the accident to read it, but perhaps it was for the best that I waited. The driver's testimony shocked me. He showed zero remorse in a way that wrenched my heart. I sobbed badly afterwards. My tears were in mourning for my blindness and naivete to the reality of a man eager to absolve himself of all blame. Was Raul protecting me from reading this all these years? The document was in his office, and he never brought it home. When I asked about it, he did bring it home but inhaled deeply as he placed it on the counter for me.

Instead of the driver saying, "I screwed up. I hit a human being, and I am sorry. Please let me help or make things better for your family," he chose to blame the sun and the unexpected appearance of an object in front of him. He claimed he thought it was a deer before his car. A deer! The memories of the struggles and upheavals I dealt with (and still deal with) came back to me. I thought about Raul and my family, who had suffered; I thought about law and justice. I wondered if things would have been different if the investigation had been more thorough if more truths about the driver's state of mind while driving had been uncovered. Had I simply been the victim of careless driving? Why had no one bothered to fight my case?

Only God knows the truth of that September day. I just sat and wept.

Again, I pictured the Life Flight landing on the helipad at Memorial Hermann and four emergency medical technicians rushing me into the emergency unit. My brain was hemorrhaging. My tongue was crushed. My pelvic bone was shattered. My tailbone and surrounding areas were broken. Everything on my right side was pretty much wrecked, including my humerus, scapula, and ribs, except, thankfully, the legs that carry me. Fortunately, my legs were not broken, but I had a big and deep scrape (road rash) all the way down my right thigh. These are forever tattooed reminders to this day.

Upon leaving TIRR, Maky recalls my short-term memory loss. Whenever the doctor told me something, she said, somebody needed to be there to listen and keep reminding me, especially in the first year. At TIRR they would give me a pad and a pencil to take notes, and I would have to write in my handwriting, which people could barely understand.

Earlier, in the years when my boys were growing, I would play off the accident in two sentences: "Mom was in a bad car accident and almost died. But the doctors saved her." Raul and I made sure to keep it simple at their young age. Plus, they really didn't need to know the gruesome details at that point in their lives. We were too busy trying to keep up with games, after school activities, homework, and regular to-dos for parents of young children. Any mom can attest to all the energy it takes to bring up a wholesome child. Every parent wishes to bring up a kind, confident, well-spirited, and loving leader. Moms need to be celebrated. Raul and I were doing the best we knew how to do to protect them as kids of a brain-injury patient. Today, they are aware of the grim details.

We had no one to guide us in bearing that cross. A friend with daughters called me once to advise: "You may want to tell Colin more about the accident. He mentioned to my girls that you got hit by a car." At the time I didn't grasp the intention behind the remark. Now it's easier to understand. Yet deciding how much detail to reveal about the accident to our boys as they were growing up was tough to navigate.

Sometimes my mind wanders—don't we all do this—thinking about the "what-ifs." What if I never signed up for that fundraising marathon in DC? What if Raul never joined me? What if it was a cloudy day? What if I ran past where the sidewalk ends thirty seconds sooner or later? What if I didn't lapse into a coma? What if I had died straight off? What if I had been unbroken? What if—we can use that for everything in life. I am now forty-six and no longer have the same energy as when I was twenty-eight. Could it be the aging process? Or is my broken body still healing?

Was it too early? Was the driver still half-asleep? Was he changing the radio station? Did he have a disagreement with his significant other? Was he distracted for a split second?

I will never know.

Only God has our plan.

What I do know is that God had this planned from the day I was born. Things happen the way they were supposed to happen. Everything happens for a reason. My husband has always been a gift—always—and it took the accident to make me fully aware. The accident brought us closer and solidified our love when it could have torn us apart instead. We hope, as people, not to wait for something bad to happen to realize our greatest gifts. But sometimes that's how it, unfortunately, goes. We both say to this day that the accident made our marriage stronger. He is testimony to the fact that, while one may hear horror stories about relationships today, there are still good people in the world.

I can't help but think of the synchronicity of life events. We all have them, even little ones, like this one: My college apartment number was 803. Years later, I would meet my husband and his home address was 803. Simple things like that make me smile. God always has his hand upon us no matter the situation.

These days Raul diligently instills in our younger son, Colin, the miracle of my recovery, and the fact that the hand of God is at work in our family. He once said to him, "You know, Colin, you're here for a reason. Your Mom had a bad car accident years ago, and she was not going to live. There's a purpose to why you are here."

Colin gazed up tearfully at Raul and waited to hear more from his Dad and hero.

"After she did make it—and that was a miracle in itself—she was told not to get pregnant. But we did, with you," continued Raul. "You are a miracle, too, and your purpose is not mediocrity. It's probably going to annoy you, but I will be on you a lot about your grades, behavior, athletics, and other things. You're not here on Earth for mediocrity," he repeated, carefully pinching his favorite wintergreen dip behind his bottom lip. The boys walked outside to fill the deer blinds with food; Mother Nature was at her finest that warm January day in south Texas.

Colin would tackle Strake Jesuit College Preparatory and become a great student, and a player on both the football and baseball teams.

I once attended Colin's "Baseball Hitathon" sponsored by Strake Jesuit in support of Gigi's Playhouse Houston, an organization supporting the Down syndrome community. The occasion reminded me of my feeling of connection to special needs communities. Speech therapy, occupational therapy, and time for fun activities at the playhouse were provided at no cost to families. Instead, expenses were covered by various grants and fundraising events, like "*Hitting a Home Run for Down Syndrome.*"

At the event, I met Cruz (a child with Down syndrome), his brother, and mother, who was nice enough to give the full background about the cause. Cruz and over thirty kids at the event had failed to let their condition slow them down. They were playing in the jump house with a slide! Again, this is a reminder, you never know what cards you will be dealt in life. Watching the moms and others put their good energies into something positive makes our world a better place.

Giving back has always been a passion seeded in me. I would say since birth and young childhood, but more so during my years of working at Texas Children's Hospital, post college. For example, I would regularly deliver gifts and toys to a local school for children in underserved communities. After my accident, and a long year in and out of rehab with endless doctor's appointments,

I made a promise to myself that I would do anything in my power to help survivors at TIRR. What could I do as a thank-you to TIRR, which had been so instrumental in my recovery? Don't ask me how, but I learned about their first ever Charity Golf Tournament in the fall of 2003. I planned to go.

At the event, I walked up the green grass to a few ladies sitting nearby. I knew no one.

"How can I help? Please put me to work," I said.

Immediately they installed me at check in, and I did my duty for a few hours. Afterwards, I wanted to know when the next one was taking place. By Monday morning, Becky Crane, one of the TIRR Family Board members, called me just as I was returning to our new Greatwood home from dropping Jacob off for preschool. I answered the phone.

"I'm calling because we would like to invite you to be on the Family board of TIRR. Would you like to join?"

Standing in the kitchen, I excitedly said, with a big smile, "Yes, of course! I would love to help. Thank you!"

Becky furnished me with details on the next meeting. This is how I initially got involved with TIRR Family. Eighteen years later, I have remained connected with TIRR. One of my founding projects was *Two Steppin' with TIRR*, created in 2014 to fundraise for brain and spinal injury research. Since I like to translate my thoughts and ideas via music, I decided to invite some country music artists.

It sounded crazy, but I just knew I could make it happen. I hoped and prayed the top administrators, Maudie and Cynthia, would go for this grandiose idea of mine. I was proposing a fundraiser to benefit brain injury and spinal-cord-injury research (spinal cord injuries take effect in your spine resulting in paralysis). For the first fundraiser, we would potentially hire country music artists Clay Walker and the late Jerry Jeff Walker. Money would be raised to benefit Mission Connect research for brain injury and spinal cord injury. Hence, it was extra meaningful because both country music artists had the last name of Walker. TBI and SCI patients will *walk* again. In subsequent years we have had the honor to host *Two Steppin' with TIRR* events with Pat Green, Tracey Lawrence, Robert Earl Keen, and John Michael Montgomery. We even stepped out of country music one year and had Kool and the Gang! Raising awareness in brain injury and spinal cord injury, with country music and other stars, would be my future. Maudie is the event planner and Cynthia is the executive director, and they make it all happen.

A favorite TIRR summer camp of mine is Moran Camp Xtreme in Brenham, Texas. It is now being offered three times a year—for fall, spring break, and summer camp. It is a camp for children aged up to twenty-one that have spinal cord injuries. Here, children have the joy of going to the no boundary camp. All the kids have so much fun with the ropes course, horseback riding, swimming, skeet shooting, and competing on one or two of the teams—Rolling Renegades or Wheeled Warriors. Only one team can be awarded the highest score. The one-mile wheelchair race always leaves me inspired—watching all the campers defeat the boundaries of their leg paralysis with the power of their arms wheeling them to victory. Definitely the most empowering, authentic experience for spinal-cord-injury patients, the week-long camp has been a uniting force for the youngsters as well as a source of comfort. I always want to stay the entire week, but volunteer help is needed for one day only. The inner grit and admiration the kids have for life no matter their disability is always inspiring. You certainly can say it puts your own priorities in place.

Fall Moran Camp Xtreme at Sea is always a must for spinal-cord-injury patients—sailing in the bay waters of Galveston Island. We, the volunteers, aid them in safely sitting in the sailboat with the help of electric ropes. Watching the joy on their faces as they sail away is always a moment of happiness that I want to share with the world.

The TIRR Family Board has been grateful for the successful fundraisers, and the not so successful ones. I've often encouraged my entire family to participate, and everyone from my siblings to parents to in-laws are always glad to do so. Even our dog, the late Maggie, contributed to TIRR in her own little way. She gave birth to ten goldens, and we gave all the profits to TIRR Hospital Mission Connect, the research team for brain and spinal cord injury. Maggie's donation became known to TIRR as a "Dog Gone Way to Give to TIRR."

Maggie, our beautiful golden retriever, deserves a book of her own. But let me begin by saying that we had first gotten her when Colin was five or six and Jacob eight. She was just the best dog that you could ever ask for. She was a human dog.

In 2019, she was diagnosed with digestive cancer. This was happening as Jacob was about to leave for college. A heavy weight came over me—a feeling of despair. My pup and my first born were both leaving me.

The next chapter in life was about to take place.

Maggie had come into our lives when we lived in Briar Grove Park. For all you dog lovers you will love this story. Raul and Jacob made regular early morning visits to the famous Houston breakfast joint the International House of Pancakes (IHOP), where Jacob would gobble down chocolate chip and regular pancakes. At a moment of lifting his fork for another tasty, doughy, and syrupy bite, Raul came across a listing in the *Houston Chronicle* for an English White Golden puppy.

The family agreed to go and look. We drove to Angelic Goldens in Magnolia, Texas. Maggie seemed like a perfect name, after Magnolia, the town in which she was born. Her parents were from Hungary in Central Europe, next door to Vienna, Austria. A perfect white was the description of this angelic pup. Maggie hopped over like a bunny and scooped up my sunglasses that had fallen under the oak tree shading us.

At that moment the entire family knew she was the pick.

A little cotton ball is what she mimicked. Raul liked her because she was the most laid-back puppy there. I liked her because she was a sweetheart, and we knew we wanted a girl because our former dog Copper had been a boy. We had given him to Raul's parents because he would just eat steaks off the counter. He was amazing in his eating talents; he actually could eat the brick off our house. I have absolutely no idea how that was remotely possible, even for a dog.

Jacob was so happy to have his new dog. Since I was mostly at home, Maggie was always with me. She needed no prompting to go outside to relieve herself. She was the easiest dog ever. A polar opposite from Copper. We had her for nine happy years till cancer struck in July, just as Jacob was getting ready to leave for his freshman year of college at the University of Colorado, Boulder.

After the diagnosis, the veterinarian removed the mass and we turned to bland diets, medications, and chemotherapy. After one chemotherapy we decided against it, as we thought it too harsh. She was still recovering from major surgery to remove the tumor in her gastric and esophageal lining; we wanted a break for her.

Our family started feeding her Juice Plus, and all of a sudden, she made a miraculous recovery. Her coat shone beautifully; we were astounded. But by mid-September, she began a downward spiral. Maggie kept vomiting, and we were confused at first because we'd just gotten the clear from the veterinarian. We took her to the ER where they conducted an ultrasound on her stomach, but forgot to check the esophageal lining, where we later learned the tumor had regrown. She had lost about ten pounds.

As she was standing and staring into my eyes, I could see her eyes saying, *Help me. I feel terrible.*

The vets felt it was best to continue care at home. They sent "Lady" Maggie, at her sickest moment, home with a protective cone around her neck to deter her from licking off her stitches. She had had surgery for the removal of her cancerous mass.

Maggie and I were benched. (I had somehow managed to break my foot—it was called the "dancer's fracture" or the break of the fifth metatarsal—as I was leaving my first writing class, taken in my aspiration to write this book.) Dad would say we were both benched. In the days of coaching soccer, he would say to a player, "Red card, you're benched."

Maggie passed on Monday, October 7, 2019.

I still dream of my angelic Maggie, happy and young. Knowing she is at Rainbow Bridge, in Heaven, always brings me comfort.

I was giving her belly rubs on the green grass. Her fur is so white, fluffy, and healthy. Not dry and old.

In the noise of life, the three-mile nature trail at Memorial Park in Houston has been my go-to running space for twenty-five years now. It could be first thing in the morning, when the sun is rising, or midday or even late evening. Regardless of the time, it has brought me much clarity and peace—it is my meditation space.

I also walk or run with my other dogs, Maggie's pups, Max and Lucy. I have to be careful with Max, though, who is of boxy build and forceful tug and can sometimes make me lose my balance. Once, while leaving the vet, my knees crashed to the ground; my bone-building calcium supplements must have saved the day because I was home free from a break! Darla from the

vet's office raced outside to check on me, then helped me to my
car while holding Max's leash. It was embarrassing though. My
mind wandered to Maggie. She was never pulling at her leash—so
dainty and ladylike. But leave it to good dog Max to add some
excitement to things.

One Monday morning, my sister-in-law, Martha, called me
first thing in the morning. I thought it must be something really
important since she never calls that early. I was going about my
normal morning routine—my run and car wash—after email-
ing Cynthia about my grandiose idea for a fundraising event for
TIRR.

Martha, whom we also call "Tita," told me on the phone
about chatting with a fellow customer at a Nordstrom's nail salon.
They exchanged information about where they lived, and this
other lady said she lived in Canyon Gate. She turned out to be
the woman who jumped over her fence to give Raul a blanket as
I lay unconscious in the middle of the road.

It was as if no time had passed as Martha told me about
her conversation. I was sucked in as though in a time warp.
Immediately I was back at that sunny September day in 2002.
Eleven years of feeling so heavy flooded me with emotions. I
sat with my feelings and allowed myself to experience all the
emotions that emerged. Many deep breaths took place. Hearing
this story only endorses my feeling of you never know who will
touch your life in the most intimate way. Her simple small act
of human kindness is recalled to this day by all of us. As I was

sitting in my car, I ran my hands through my hair in disbelief at the coincidence. What are the odds of running into this lady? Especially at the Nordstrom nail salon, in the city of millions in Houston. People are ultimately good in our world no matter all the disturbing news stories we hear day in and day out. We need to hear more of the good ones. As I continued to run my hands through my hair pondering the coincidence, suddenly I noticed my hair was due for another round of highlights.

Fabrice, my hairstylist to this day, would say that after my accident, he saw that I had the will to survive. The family had had to make appointments on my behalf with him. I'd earlier missed an appointment while in coma, and Fabrice had not heard from me till my family contacted him. They briefed him in order to prepare him for the shock of seeing me.

"Hi Fabrice," I said, opening the door in our long hallway, with my mother and Pauline holding me up. I wore a black patch over my eye. I was talking slowly and quietly. I noticed him trying not to act surprised with my new appearance and slow movements.

He did my hair in the master bedroom. Our conversation was in slow motion, like the slo-mo app on an iPhone. Today, as we reminisce and he is folding my hair in the highlighted foil, Fabrice tells me in his French accent, "I knew you were not yourself, but you always had a smile on your face."

As I look over the balcony from my patio, I see the sea, but it is not the Sea of Marmara, a northeastern extension of the Mediterranean Sea that separates Asian Turkey from the European side of Turkey. It is Lake Travis in Austin, Texas.

Sitting on the lakeside patio circles me back to the seventies and days growing up on Burgaz Island, which is one of the Princes' Islands located in the Sea of Marmara, near Istanbul, Turkey. That is where my paternal grandparents had their summer home, where their island house was situated. From the view of my grandmother's patio, you could see Spoon Island, set between Burgaz and Heybeliada islands across the way. No one lives on Spoon Island. It's a small, beautiful island, and I was reminded of it as I gazed across Lake Travis to the distant shoreline that shows the continuum of land across the waters.

The view takes me back to childhood. Such a calming, secure time. Cool breezes and the comfort of grandparents, aunts, uncles, and cousins at the house on the island. My grandmother's art studio at the island house was where everything was secure and comfortable. It was also where she would give us painting lessons as children. I always watched with great interest on her artistic ability. As a child, I always wondered what it was that had invited her to such creativity. Each of her carefully brushed strokes were always meticulous placed onto the painting. What was she thinking? You could see the intent as well as her eyes mesmerized knowing her exact placement of each brushed stroke of the paint. Sometimes and automatically, as she would douse one color with another, she was in her zone and on autopilot, knowing exactly her finish line. I loved to watch her intense work of art come to life. I wanted to be good at art, but my creativity was stirring inside of me in a different way, though I was always curious about what her next painting would be. My creativity comes out in music and other visual works of art.

Days would be spent going to the beach and relaxing in the evenings with my parents, grandparents, aunts, and uncles playing backgammon. The ladies would be chatting away on the couch or on the outdoor patio at the kitchen table. Mornings would be full of fresh cherek, fresh bread, feta cheeses, Turkish coffee, hot tea … and I can't forget the black Kalamata olives.

Before breakfast, Brother and I would run about a mile down from Kristinmama's to the local bakery at the lower end of the island. We would holler in Turkish, "iki ekmek," asking for two loaves through a little glass sliding window. They would hand us the freshly baked, hot bread, and the aroma would flood our noses and the streets. A yeasty and buttery smell made our mouth water, and we would sprint it back up to the island home. Sometimes Brother and I would stop and eat some on the way back home.

Everything was within walking distance, or, if not, a horse and carriage were waiting. A simple way of life it was, and still is today. Although my Aunt and Uncle continue to live on Burgaz Island, they recently informed me that mini taxis have overtaken the horse and carriage lifestyle. We must go back to the original way of life. The horse and carriages on the Princes' Islands were a hidden gem.

After our holidays were over, we would travel to my grand-parents' house in Istanbul, where my paternal grandmother, Kristinmama, lived. We were at the Tatas (our great-aunts' house) where they made homemade lemonade for all of us grandkids. The lights in the apartment were dim; there were cozy couches of mustard color with stripes, and off-white walls with big, thick linen curtains. We would all celebrate being together with glasses of delicious, freshly squeezed lemonade, by our Tatas.

My Kristinmama was very special to me, especially because I was named after her. A painter, sculptor, and mother of three, Kristin Saleri was a prominent twentieth-century Turkish artist of Armenian descent. She was a child prodigy.

My grandmother was apolitical yet remained undeterred by the huge hurdles of being a female-minority artist in a period of social and ethnic strain in post–World War II Turkey. She became a leading force in the Turkish art community as co-founder of the International Turkish Female Artists Association and co-chair of the Turkish Painters Association, using her art to convey a message of modern feminism.

Kristinmama was inspired by all aspects of Armenian culture, but she had wide ranging interests in other cultures as well, which I think has influenced me. I love to travel and experience new cultures.

"Cathedral" By Kristin Saleri
1970

Surrounded by some of my grandmother's paintings throughout my life has given me great comfort and inspiration during my
recovery, and still today. Her painting titled "Cathedral" inspires
a feeling of adoration.

My paternal grandfather, Hagopdede (or Hagop Salerian)
was an electrical and mechanical engineer by training. Being an
entrepreneur, he played an instrumental role in the industrializa-
tion of Turkey in the 1950s and 1960s. Going back further in my
family tree, my great-great-uncle, Rupen Sevag—a poet, writer,
Lieutenant in the Turkish Army, and medical doctor—was tar-
geted for deportation in the first major event of the Armenian
genocide in 1915 known as "Red Sunday."

He did not survive.

As the sun brightened the Turkish skies during summer days,
my brother Sy, Hagopdede, and I would go down the winding
hill trail to the Marmara Sea for our weekly mussel collecting.

Once we came down the dirt path, we lightly stepped on the jagged white rocks along the shoreline. I recall my Dede's stomach hanging over his swim shorts. Sy and I would wear our green swimsuits from the Neptunes. I always carried my grandmother's colorful beach bag, which held our swim towels. The lukewarm temperature of the navy-colored Marmara Sea was always inviting. Walking over the white rocks we were sure to lift our feet or try to walk softly on them, since we threw off our flip flops as we set our towels and bag down. At the shoreline we would dive in for a quick swim, and diving under the sea, Hagop Dede would lead us over to the magical rock that held an abundance of mussels. One by one we collected and filled a bucket he'd brought along. A memory so simple, it brings me joy remembering it today.

That afternoon we brought our fresh mussels up to Kristinmama, who would start to marinate them with a touch of salt, wine-vinegar, and other potent yet tasty spices. She would boil them to perfect tenderness and taste while we sat in the next room, where the tiled fireplace bearing Kristinmama's art gave off an intense smoky aroma. Kristinmama and Aunt Rehan, Dad's sister, and Mom were always cooking fulfilling meals, especially when we brought up the mussels from the sea. Turkish news was always blaring in the background while my uncle and Dad would be playing backgammon.

When my mother was six and ready to go to grade school, her parents, Papu and Takumama, decided not to send her to a Turkish school as was required by the government. My grandfather ended up making a deal with the Italian Catholic school of the nuns of Ivrea, or Scuola Italiana Delle Suore D'Ivrea, as was inscribed on the plaque next to the entrance on the exterior wall.

Ivrea was a town northwest of Milan.

It must have been September 1955. The nuns ran a very strict curriculum, and the school had its own chapel integrated among the classrooms on the second floor. The students had to study both in Italian and Turkish in most courses. My mother clearly remembers the excitement of being there. Takumama and Papu were people with a strong sense of culture. They enjoyed playing Bezique, the French card game from the nineteenth century for two players.

Takumama loved to sing, so anytime she would sing Mom would know she was in a good mood.

Papu had inherited his father's business, Lazarovich Ship Chandlers, which provided goods of any kind for large ships and oil tankers that were traveling in the Bosporus. They would go to church during religious holidays. In the open-air market bazaar, where the Armenian church was located, my Mom would stop by during shopping to light a candle or two and say a prayer.

It was the summer of 1966. Mom and her nuclear family had just settled into their little summer house high up on the fourth largest island. It was a ten- to twenty-minute boat ride from Burgaz Island. Mom was to have her fun-filled summer with her best friend Ada on the big island. Soon after they moved in, they found out that the much larger house down below them, with the same beautiful garden, was going to be occupied by another family with twin brothers and an older sister. Mom and Ada became very curious.

A few days later they heard whistling, and they saw two young boys below the window. Takumama was not pleased at all with this approach to meeting and reprimanded the boys. A few days later, once Takumama realized it was a good Armenian family, she relaxed more. That was the beginning. The two boys were Uncle and a friend of the twins. The second twin had not arrived yet. He was in the city taking his entrance exams for Robert College.

The following weekend, July 26th, all the kids went to the pier to welcome Uncle's twin, Dad, who was arriving by boat from the city. Mom was there to meet the twin's brother. The ferry boat docked. Boat propellers rotated loud acoustic sounds. The exhausts steamed as the foghorn blew. A few minutes later, Dad walked off the wooden bridge that connected boat to land and joined his brother and friends. Dad was wearing his dark suit, as he was looking his best for Robert College.

Mom and Dad began their love story under the small tower clock on the big island, where friends would all gather to chat. Dad spoke perfect English, Armenian, and Turkish so he could communicate with my mother who spoke Greek, Armenian, Turkish, English, French, and Italian fluently. Fifty-four years later, Mom and Dad continue celebrating their life together!

Having such distinguished parents, I have sometimes wondered what life would have held for me if I had pursued my academic path to the fullest. Academics have always been hard for me. In my forty-fourth year of life, I was diagnosed with ADHD. I always think about what an incredible difference knowing this would have made in my academic life—if I had known this in my school-aged years. Such knowledge would have presented me with tools to better deal with my academics and mental concentration. Although, I recently learned that ADHD can be residual effect of a brain injury. I now wonder if it was truly there in my early school years, or whether it only became prominent after the accident. Regardless, I share this in hopes that any brain injury survivor can get tested for it, and if necessary, educate themselves about ADHD and learn how to properly manage it. Again, it's never too late.

My friend Heather believes I was changed after the accident too. In short, everyone thinks the same.

"Maybe more empathetic?" Heather would say today.

"You're nicer. You're just nicer," Raul says.

I've sometimes wondered to myself, "God, what kind of person was I?" But then I think people hopefully evolve with age. I was young and immature. Thank God we didn't have social media in the 80s and 90s when I was growing up. Being a kid today is tough and no doubt about that. Again, if all of us parents know how to manage the social media world today and give our kids the proper guidance it will all be okay in our fast-moving lifestyles.

Today a question arose: "If the car accident happened to someone else, what would your response be?"

My immediate answer was "How in the world did you do it? How did you raise children and run the family at the same time? How did you mentally and physically heal? How much guilt did you carry for the friends and family witnessing you struggle for life? Did you ever feel survivor's guilt? Did you experience post-trauma? Did family or friends experience post-trauma? How did or does this affect your life today?" Let me answer these intimate questions for you.

Even though it has been eighteen years, I still do not diminish the time.

I never will.

I kept moving and looking forward. That is all you can do. Looking back will not get you anywhere. Sometimes you have to know darkness to see the light. Keep looking at today and tomorrow. Keep the faith even when it feels quite dark, as God has an ultimate and mysterious plan. The support of my lovely husband, family and friends, and my own inner faith made it happen. No if, ands, or buts, this is how it happened.

Post trauma, I feel like I have talked about everything to the deepest core. Everything is out in the open and I am sharing my story to help others. This is my duty. I am positive my accident took place in order to help others or at least to be an inspiration. We all should share our stories and make the world a better place. Every day, for one reason or another, I remember what happened. This grounds me. If I worry about silly stuff, I remind myself: Someone always has it worse, maybe lying in a hospital bed unconscious, someone can't walk, someone is hurting, someone is depressed, someone is battling addiction, anything, the list goes on. My fate was unknown. We don't have to have a trauma, cancer, etc. for us to see this reality. We were all put on Earth for a reason—let's all make it a good reason.

As I approach the end of my story, I would like to address a question I've often run into, and which I suspect is on every reader's mind. My OB-GYN had once asked me the same question too.

"I've been meaning to ask you this," he said in a serious tone. "Did you have a near-death experience?" At that exact moment his cell phone rang. It was his daughter, also named Kristin, calling. Call it what you will or call it synchronicity.

I was taken aback and a little unsure of how to reply. I had experienced something during the coma. But where had I been? What had happened? I had experienced vivid dreams. But what was I to call them? Maybe God and his angels on the other side decided I wasn't ready and sent me back to our world.

"Honestly, something happened," I replied. "But I don't know what, as I'm not the same person I was before the accident. I cannot explain it, but I see everything in a different light now. Everything."

I am forever grateful to God for every
Sunrise.

"Do not go where the path may lead, go instead
where there is no path and leave a trail."
Ralph Waldo Emerson

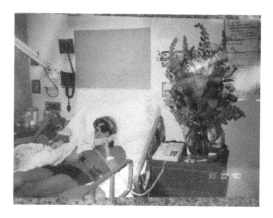

TIRR Hospital

Me

2002

TIRR Camp Xtreme Racing with Camper

2018

TIRR Camp Xtreme Treehouse
Camper and Myself
2018

TIRR Camp Xtreme Treehouse
Pauline and Camper
2018

Our Wedding Day
2000

Our Family
Jacob, Myself, Raul and Colin
2021

TIRR Camp Xtreme at Sea
2016

TIRR Camp Xtreme Race
2018

Sailboats
By Kristin Saleri
1978

Epilogue

A Fresh Perspective

It was difficult telling my story, as many memory gaps came into play. However, even with the gaps, the effect of the incident is forever ingrained in my body, flesh, and bones. From the day of the accident, and throughout the first year, I have battled memory loss, especially short-term.

My friend Rachelle and I have interviewed family and friends to help fill in the blanks. Some names in the book have been altered to protect the privacy of the individuals; but for the ones truly named, I have used their real identities here with their permission.

During both my stay in the hospital and outpatient therapy, I have come to realize best practices that have proved even more beneficial for a quicker and more pleasant recovery. I am sure that things are different from when I had the accident eighteen years ago. Hospital practices have improved as well. My personal thoughts are offered below, and while I do not mean to take away from the wonderful work being done by medical professionals at the front lines, I hope that my few words as a former patient may add to the larger picture.

My top tips and suggestions (no particular order, all are number one):

1. Please interview patients quarterly and at least once a year post accident. The patient's discharge does not mean healing is complete. I was well enough to go home but having some monthly, quarterly, bi-annual, and annual tracking system would have been beneficial. In person would be the best. Now that we are in the time of Zoom, a Zoom call would be beneficial as well. However, there were many variables that played a role in my out-of-hospital experiences. Motherhood, broken bones, neurological functions, trying to "look" normal when battling inside, etc. were issues taking place at the same time for me. It is a forever injury.

2. Have an outdoor atrium in the hospital or take the patient outside at least once a day. The fresh air, healing soil microbes, and sight of nature are a blessing for patients. It is possible that some hospitals do this now, but it was different during my time. Doctors and nurses, please, you must let your patient outside. If the outdoors is off regulations, take the patient out to a patio or balcony or at least open the windows.

I remember "sneaking" out once (I guess we can call it that). I really wanted to get a breath of fresh air. This was with my sister, Pauline, in my hospital room. I felt claustrophobic. Pauline saw the desperation in my eyes. I needed to get out and smell the fresh air. Outside I would feel free. Pauline knew it was wrong but helped me down the elevator anyway. I took big, deep breaths as I sat outside. We remained in the garden for a few minutes before a nurse saw us and asked my sister to take me back into the building. Thank you, little Sis, those brief minutes were a blessing.

3. Every patient is different. It would be helpful to prepare a physical and mental test to see what physical action that patient is capable of doing based on their level of recovery. Similar patients should be placed in related activity groups slated for both morning and afternoon sessions. I say this is because I remember most of my rehab activities were in the mornings.

4. I needed more speech therapy, which was only provided to me when I was in TIRR. When I got home, sometimes I was misunderstood because of my slurred speech. This wasn't as big of a need as my walking and balance priorities, but I believe my speech would have recovered faster if I had had a continued therapy program in that area. To this day, I still have subtle speech issues. Raul is the only one who notices it, though. To this end, professionals should kindly provide more monitoring and testing of speech progression and add more therapy sessions to the overall recovery regimen.

5. How about paintings or art on the ceilings? All of us patients are continuously looking straight up, usually at the lovely vinyl tile or the popcorn ceiling. How about we make paintings of nature, the sky, or something intriguing and inviting on the ceilings? It could be a simple inspirational image of someone walking again. Even inspirational quotes and/or positive affirmations.

6. At discharge, a trauma psychotherapist should be assigned to both the patient and family members. A therapist should walk hand in hand with the patient and family for the first year.

Dr. Francisco had me referred to a therapist, and it helped me tremendously. However, I have wished that my family had the benefit of a therapist to help with the healing and overall coping process. To this day, my parents and husband are very protective when I'm outside running, as they should be. However, proper counseling can work through these steps of unnecessary tension, fear and nervousness. They have avoided eating at the same Italian restaurant we went to before the day of my accident. My husband won't let me walk the dogs on the side of the road next to oncoming cars, and my younger sister is still nervous when I call from Raul's phone.

7. Provide Uber or transportation to patients in need of such services. Begin a fundraiser for people in need of financial assistance for this.

8. Media and Hollywood representations of brain-injury realities could be better. There are extreme situations represented where the patients are either super intelligent after the injury or impaired and defective. It is possible for the brain to heal back to its original state, and we need to be aware of this. The individual can be put back together again to a state of normalcy, where they regain their previous life without intensely dramatic aftermaths. My all-time favorite movie is Concussion with Dr. Bennet Omalu.

9. More excellent no-boundaries camps are needed for special needs or brain- and spinal-cord-injury patients. Part of the profits from sales of this book will go into efforts at setting up more

camps and supporting continued research by TIRR Memorial Hermann and Mission Connect for brain and spinal cord injuries.

10. It is important to check for possible corollary conditions like diabetes insipidus. I was drinking so much fluid after being discharged that Dr. Brandon Gunn, my dear friend's husband, thankfully noticed. There can be many secondary injuries to brain injury. Navigating post TBI, be aware that it is not unusual to come across the following:

Physical	Cognitive	Behavioral
Paralysis	Depression	Inappropriate behavior
Coordination Problems	Disorganization	Tiredness
Convulsions	Disrupted Sleep	Lack of Self-Awareness
Sexual Impairment	Emotionality	Loss of Empathy
	ADHD	Irritability
	Confusion	Bewilderment
	Impaired Language Skills	Exhaustion
	Loss of abstract understanding, reading/writing	
	Headaches and impaired vision	

Good News: There likely are doctors or specialists a patient can work with to further improvements and healing in each specific area.

11. I both loved and appreciated the organization of my daily schedules on the whiteboard. It encouraged me and helped me map the progress of my baby steps in getting better.

12. Sticky notes are a must tool for outpatient caregivers, especially when the patient first arrives home. It sets reminders of things spoken, things to do, memory cues, missed directions, and so on. Reading everything twice or more is a good habit to start, too. It helps the brain rewire faster in the first year of home recovery. With our iPhones and other technologies today, reminders can be made—set alarms and timers on your smart phone. According to the *Journal of the International Neuropsychological Society*, about 64 percent of patients recover cognitively in the first year. I however believe this percentage could be higher if patients were inundated with visual aids every step of the way.

13. Experiencing frustration is normal for the patient upon arrival at home, and it is vital to prepare family and caretakers for the new reality. The patient will be eager to get back to normal and take on everything. Health staff should kindly prepare and have a plan for family and caretakers to adhere by and implement. Prescribing a post-brain-injury life coach to the patient will be optimal.

14. Please talk to the patient in a coma. You may naturally think they don't hear you, but they do. Trust me, talking to the patient helps. Tell stories—good stories, funny stories, all kinds of stories. Touching and holding the patient sustains that familiarity with the world they've always known. Recognizable smells and sounds can go a long way.

15. There have been proven benefits of Yoga, and Tai Chi for victims of head and brain injury. Personally, I am more of a hot yoga fan. Again, it's your own personal opinion—all are great. Remember that they all have health benefits. It is important to incorporate this into the recovery program where a safe, peaceful space and conscious breathing practices are emphasized. It also helps in restoring body alignment and managing the effects of overstimulation. It clears neural pathways for better thinking.

16. Do not talk to a brain-injury patient in a childish manner. Speak to them as you would normally do. Depending on the patient, he or she can understand and relate to you in accordance with their age. It leads me to recall my loving grandmother-in-law, who was filled with quick, witty humor and always laughed with me. Abita, as we all called her, was always stylishly dressed. She loved to play bridge. She related to me as the adult she had always known. Abita will always hold a special place in my heart. She gave me an angel to keep by my hospital bed; I have held onto it for years. Abita you are always my angel.

17. Doctors, please share with caregivers, in layman's terms, which parts of the brain are damaged and what is to be expected or not expected in the continued healing process. Specifically define what that entails. This will be very helpful to the caregivers and patient.

18. Find a support group for the patient and patient caregiver. Having support every step of the way is the key to success for anything. The last thing a patient wants is to feel alone in their journey to recovery.

19. As we all are aware, exercise makes the heart pump blood faster and the brain is the biggest consumer of oxygen. Aerobic exercise (running, walking, swimming, and biking) helps prepare, protect, and repair brain cells and grow new ones. It's the best for brain health. It will help the head space feel sharp, you will feel the oxygen pumping to your brain and clarifying your pathways. Studies show that movement helps lower memory loss and chances of developing Alzheimer's disease, to which brain-injury patients are more susceptible.

Therefore, exercise is golden. Try your local gym or a personal trainer (if you can afford one). I was lucky enough to have my spouse support me during workouts. If that is not available to you, please find a friend or ask a family member, neighbor, or caretaker to assist you during your exercise. You need someone to monitor *you*. Make this a priority. When my husband took me to the local track, I started with baby steps, literally speaking. I would walk a quarter of the track and go a step further the next time. There were times I would not be able to proceed and would have to rest. I was finally able to walk or jog the 5k at the Houston Marathon in 2003.

Start with a once a week, then bump it up from there a few times a week. Baby steps. In other words, take it slow. No need to hurry, as recovery from TBI is a marathon, not a sprint. Trying to make too much progress too soon could end up in unnecessary disaster. Be easy on *you*. I am sharing what I have learned over the past eighteen years of recovery and can only advise you based on my experience. Please, always consult your doctor or your trained expert with any eating or exercise regime, especially post injury.

20. Use daily prayer and affirmations. Focus on goals you or loved ones make for you. Always have a daily quote of inspiration to lead you.

21. Listen to *your* body.

22. Take up a new hobby, perhaps a musical instrument. Check out Gabby Giffords online at pbs.org. She is using music to rewire her brain after being shot. Gabby is an example of true grit and determination.

23. Meditate (find the perfect spot in your home or in nature). I personally try to do this every day or most days. Many scientific studies suggest that mindfulness meditation improves focus, reduces stress, and helps with anxiety and depression.

24. Keeping a journal. Write, write and write some more. This is meant to do when the Brain Injury Patient is home from the hospital. Write from your room, your backyard, waiting in the carpool line and anywhere your heart desires, too much writing can never happen. If you feel uneasy about it, throw it away! Or if worried someone will see it throw it in a fire or put through a paper shredder. Crumple it. Do away with it. Or simply keep in your journal. Get it out somewhere. Big to do for me. I love to write things down, particularly to remember things as well as for therapeutic reasons. As I wrote this book, it became a very unintentional therapeutic process.

25. Hire a professional organizer. If this is not financially do-able, please have a family member, friend, neighbor or someone

from your Church Community to help with this. It is a game changer in the road to recovery. A right-hand man committed to you to help keep you focused and organized.

This now brings me to the wonderful community of people who helped me at several times, and who have not been mentioned so far. I would like to graciously thank them for their love and timeless support. They are:

My caring wheelchair "driver" at TIRR was Jeri, a dear friend from college who was always there in those times during my recovery. I had met her in college back when we were eighteen. We laughed together and always went to the same college gatherings. She wheeled me to bingo, hence I call her "driver" here. April Muckleroy was another close and dear friend in college. How could I have gotten to this point without you? I am forever grateful for our friendship. Keri Norman, a big sister in the sorority and dear friend. Jamie Morris was another friend in college, and we went to University of Hawaii together to play golf and get a credit for SFA. Heather Mahan was always a best friend. Thank you all for being there for me. Always.

My nearest and dearest Aunt and Uncle that are forever by my side, my Aunt Judi, Uncle Nonik (Alen), Aunt Rehan and Uncle Bernard, I love you forever. Uncle Nonik was my running coach who helped me run my first half-marathon nine months post-accident. Ara, my cousin who forever talks about how I inspire him. You are also an inspiration to me, Ara. He laughs at the same jokes as me. We are one of the same, personality-wise. Gregory, I love you and always admire your love and dedication to family and work. Justin was another close cousin he is now a neurologist in New Orleans. Watching all my male cousins grow into family men always makes me smile. Chloe is my very lovely baby cousin; she is the youngest of my cousins. I am so proud of the young lady you have become and new wife. I can't wait to see what God has planned for you and David. I love each one of you for own special reasons.

And of course, I will restate Ophelia here, even though I have mentioned her in previous pages. Ofi was an angel to me with a heart of gold. She drove me everywhere, catered to me, and provided companionship to both I and Jacob. She was a helper during my continuation of the activities of daily living. Where would I be without you by my side? Endless Thank You to dear Ofi.

Activities of daily living, or ADLs, are basic tasks that must be accomplished every day for an individual to thrive. ADLs include personal hygiene tasks such as bathing, grooming, oral care, nail care, and hair care. There was a shower chair sitting in the shower in my TIRR bathroom. I would sit on it and let the hot water run through my hair. Although I was alone in the bathroom, I am sure my husband or Mom were right at the door peeking in and checking on me.

The first couple weeks at TIRR, I needed help with anything to do with personal hygiene. Someone always walked with me to the bathroom and helped me to sit on the toilet. I recall wanting so badly to do it on my own, but apparently, my brain was not firing signals quick enough to my legs. The good news was that by the third week I was able to use the restroom on my own.

Dressing was the same thing as using the restroom. I learned to lace my shoes like a preschool child. After daily showers at TIRR, Mom would help me get ready for the day or put on pajamas (depending on the time of day). Showering and dressing could take as long as two hours. This kept on up until three months post-accident. With time, I was able to pick and choose proper clothes for different occasions. As time passed I slowly but surely got use to the new normal.

In the first few weeks, I needed assistance with eating and had to relearn how to hold a spoon correctly. Ambulation in terms of ADL involved a person's ability to change from one position to the other and to walk independently. Before I was finally discharged at TIRR, Keri the nurse had to run me through a series of tests involving lying on the bed and getting up or getting into the passenger seat of a car. Again, any caregiver being family or friend is a must for help after discharge. Please plan accordingly or have your patient advocate help organize this.

Instrumental activities of daily living (IADLs) are somewhat more complex, but nevertheless also reflect on a person's ability to live independently and thrive. IADLs are measured by things such as transportation and shopping. In other words, how well a person can procure grocery and pharmacy needs without help. Preparing meals was also another IADL factor, although Mom, Pauline, Ofi, caring school friends from St. Laurence Catholic School, neighbors, and friends were handy at this time of need.

During this day and age, we are lucky. There is more easy access to help than ever before, especially with Mobile Apps, Instacart, Uber Eats, and Door Dash, just to name a few. Please use resources to help with shopping and Uber for transportation.

Various aspects of household management were considered as well. Mom, Popi, Ofi and Carolina cleaned, tidied up, removed trash and clutter, and did laundry. There were other considerations, like managing medications (getting prescriptions filled, keeping medications up-to-date, and taking meds on time and in the right dosages), communicating with others, and handling the household's phones, mail, and general appearance—making the home hospitable and welcoming for visitors. Again, please hire help if needed. If there are financial hardships, please be sure to ask family or friends—people are very giving in a time of need.

Managing finances was also a big part, although I was lucky that Raul always took care of that. It was important to monitor how much assistance a person would need in managing bank balances, checkbooks, and paying bills on time. I will say it again, please hire appropriate help, such as a financial advisor, or ask family, friends, or neighbors to help with this one.

This is a must…Please keep exercise or movement logs. Specifically have your caregiver grab a journal at Office Depot or the nearest office supply store. There are plenty of great apps to use, too. Utilizing something to track your daily, weekly and/ or monthly goals is always very motivational to the patient. It's awesome to see any progress or how much improvement has taken place over time. Phones today have many apps, too. Record exercise and your rehab process with an app, or write it down, the old school way, in a journal.

I like to go back and look at the log that I had kept at the time.

By Christmas Day of December 2002, I'd started keeping a log of my physical progress. It was no accident that I started on this day, as Christmas is my favorite holiday. This was my and Raul's daily ritual at the time, as he would coach me to walk or run at the Fort Bend High School track. My log at the time is as follows:

12/26/02 1-mile run, walk 3 laps/run 1 lap
12/27/02 PT with #4 weights

12/28/02 15 push-ups, 25 sit-ups, 3 miles/run1 lap

12/29/02 Bicep curl, tricep extension 2x15x, 16 push-ups, 25 sit-ups, 18 min. Pilates

12/30/02 Bike 16 min., push-ups 15x, sit up 25, 15 min. Pilates, Physical Therapy

12/31/02 25 Sit-ups, 15 min. Pilates/Physical Therapy

1/3/03 25 Sit-ups, 2x15 bicep curl, 2x25 bicep extension, 2 miles 25:29

The log goes on till January 22, 2003.

At this point, I would like to leave a few words expressing my sound thoughts on mental health awareness and my own personal progress with therapy sessions. The reason for this added emphasis is to relay how my writing of this book has helped me realize the truth in the words of Martha Mealey, my therapist, who believes that time doesn't matter. It is never too late to talk about trauma.

I was talking to her one day from the gray couch when my eyes welled up with tears. Grief overcame me, maybe for the first time. I had finally processed the accident. I wished I had known of the grief-trauma disconnection that was present through the years as I was bringing up two boys in a hamster-wheel-type lifestyle. I knew I wanted to talk about everything, but I didn't know how or couldn't put my thoughts in order.

My original therapist, post TIRR, had a wonderful listening ear, and she did her best to keep me stable. After one year, I thought I no longer needed further care and stopped going. The keyword here is "thought"—I should have continued, just as my husband and both of our family's should have continued some path of emotional care as well. This was a traumatic experience for all.

I got used to quickly reciting my story, scared of boring people with too many details. "I was running with my husband. The sun was in the driver's eyes, and he hit me going 25 mph. Coma for seven days. It's all good; I'm here today."

I would usually say this in a ten-second spiel. "A blessing," I would say.

However, as Martha Mealey explained to me, our brains and bodies shut down to protect us from pain. Even my husband does not remember some parts of my story. This raises the question of undergoing hypnosis, but I feel that would be prying too much into what God has chosen to make us forget.

With any trauma or death, I would say that grief is healthy and expected. Especially in the sense that you are losing the old you. The stages of grief—which were made popular by Elizabeth Kubler-Ross in her 1969 book *On Death and Dying*—has yielded a lot of insight for me. According to Kubler-Ross, the stages are denial and isolation; anger; bargaining/if-only statements; depression; and finally, acceptance. These stages are explained in detail on online websites, and it is best to research them carefully in order to understand them fully. However, I am relieved to say that I went through these stages.

The best thing we can do is allow ourselves to feel the grief as it comes over us. Resisting it only prolongs the natural healing. In the past year and a half of focusing my energies on the writing of this book, I have come to understand acceptance. I have found more awareness of my brain-injury trauma this past year. I originally came into this book writing process to help other patients, families and friends to manage their own brain injury. In the end, writing ultimately healed me. Writing and discussing topics day in and day out made me aware of the unseen trauma I was dealt.

Feel your deep-seated pain.

Time doesn't matter.

Please hire a counselor or therapist. Both for the patient and any family member or friend involved in the loss of the brain injury patient. The loss is real of the person who we are before and after traumatic brain injury. Mental health awareness is a must.

There has also been the problem of the well-known "survivor's guilt"—feeling horrible for surviving a catastrophic accident that you had absolutely no control over—which I have experienced. When I hear stories of non-survivors who happen to be people I know, either personally or through family or friends, I sometimes think, *Why me? Why did I live and not them?* I feel terribly guilty. Now, I circle back and share with you that it is okay to be empathetic for people but also, at the same time, know that your journey is your journey. This was my own personal journey of life on Earth, which God has led me through. Everyone has their own highway to Heaven.

Maggie's Puppies 2013

Tree of Life
By Kristin Saleri
1985

Useful Resources

- tirrfoundation.org. To follow education on research and medical science, improvements in care, and life enhancement for people with traumatic brain and spinal cord injuries. To follow current camp dates at TIRR, check out tirrfoundation.org/youth-programs
- memorialhermann.org
- Brain Injury Association of America: http://www.biausa.org/
- Brainline.org: www.brainline.org
- Brain Injury Resource Center: www.headinjury.com
- Defense and Veterans Brain Injury Center: https://dvbic.dcoe.mil
- Centers for Disease Control: Injury Prevention and Control: Traumatic Brain Injury: https://www.cdc.gov/traumaticbraininjury/index.html
- Family Caregiving Alliance: https://www.caregiver.org/traumatic-brain-injury
- The American Physical Therapy Association, which lists resources directed toward wounded warriors and their caregivers: http://www.apta.org/TBI/

Other Organizational Resources

- TraumaticBrainInjury.com has organized a state-by-state guide for those seeking information about local resources. They can be found at: https://www.traumaticbraininjury.com/ resources/
- Oprah's "Super Soul Sunday" programs are filled with inspirational series that nourish the mind, body, and spirit.

Readings

A book I love to carry by my side is *Lent with Saint Teresa of Calcutta* by Heidi Hess Saxton. Although this book of daily meditations is for the season of Lent, I love to read it on an everyday basis. Dr. Maya Angelou's words of wisdom always speak to me and she is another favorite author of mine. Her life work and inspiration is worth mentioning. I love this one from The Catholic Company: "Starting the morning off with God is the key to strength and success in your day."

Other favorites are the books of Brene Brown, such as *Dare to Lead*, *Daring Greatly*, *Gifts of Imperfection*, and *Braving the Wilderness*. A favorite quote from Brene Brown: "One day you will tell your story of how you overcame what you went through, and it will be someone else's survivors guide." Thank you Brene Brown!

Elizabeth Gilbert's *Eat, Pray, Love* is likewise inspirational. Cheryl Strayed's *Brave Enough* always reminds me of the need for resilience. I love her quote that says, "Love many, trust few, and always paddle your own canoe."

Other worthwhile books are *Glass Castle* by Jeannette Walls, Glennon Doyle's *Love Warrior* and Paul Young's *The Shack*. Lee and Bob Woodruff's *In an Instant* and Eckhart Tolle's *The Power of Now* remain much-loved picks.

Acknowledgements

A special and deep thank-you to those on the front lines that helped save my life. You are all heroes, and I was gifted life because of you. Especially the Fire Station in Richmond, TX. You helped make my survival a fact. Words do not speak enough for my gratitude. Thank you to all the frontline workers: the emergency care team at the accident site, Life Flight on September 29, 2002, Memorial Hermann Emergency Medical Center, Memorial Hermann ICU doctors, TIRR doctors, TIRR hospital, and all the physical therapists, occupational therapists, and every doctor that help saved my life, especially Dr. Francisco. Thank you, Cynthia Adkins and Becky Crane, for welcoming me with open arms to the TIRR Family in 2003. An endless thank-you to Judith, Craig, and all the caregivers at Polly Ryon in continuing and completing my physical therapy to the fullest after TIRR.

I owe my life to my steadfast husband—Raul you stood by me every step of the way; Thank You for holding me tight. I will love you forever. My deepest treasures aka "my boys," Jacob and Colin, thank you for being you and growing into wonderful young men. Keep dreaming big dreams. They will come true. To Mom and Dad, you are my indomitable heroes. Thank you for giving me life. Uncle Nonik, how can I thank you for your rich medical knowledge, love, and support during my journey? To

Maky and Carlos, I am lucky enough to have another set of parents—you! May the sun of hope and blessings continue to shine on you. You were and are my forever heroes and never would let me fall. I will love you forever. My siblings, Sy and Selin, Pauline and Chris, Tita and Dan, and April and Payo—you are the diamonds of my heart. I love each of you. Kelly Borally thank you for being a loyal friend. I was lucky to find a friend like you. All my nieces and nephews, Daniel, Patrick, Anna, Carlos, and Mia, I am so proud to be your aunt and so proud of the young adults you have become.

To all my near and dear friends—Heather Gunn, Keely Krhovjak, Erica Yeary, Heather Mahan and all the Yaya Sisters and their families—you will always have a special place in my heart. Some are silver and some are gold ... all of you are my number ones. Thank You! There are too many people to mention, and I have already noted them in the book. I hold you all in my heart forever.

Thank you, Dr. Francisco for your lifelong commitment in saving lives and saving my life. Thank You, TIRR Mission Connect and all the scientists for your ongoing research for brain injury and spinal cord injury. Thank You to TIRR Family and TIRR Hospital for saving my life and your forever support in making lives better and saving lives every day.

Thank you, Elizabeth LaGrone, for bringing me hope and being a listening ear during my first-year post brain injury. Martha Mealey, the amazing therapist, who made me more aware of me. I genuinely thank you with all my heart.

Thank you, Laura Hynes-Keller, for making my dream come true! For believing in me and making me aware that I have a voice. This book is a reality because of you. I couldn't have done this without you.

Thank you to my editor, Dr. Onyinye Ihezukwu—I was lucky enough to have you! Thank you for your commitment, patience, and hard work and especially for your time. You are too kind, and your writing talent is amazing. You taught me so much. Your non-fiction class at Inprint in summer 2019 was nothing but inspiring and launched me into writing my story.

Thank You to my Archway Editors, you perfected what I was trying to say! Thank You for all your time and energy with me.

Thank you, Mrs. Nancy Geyer, for your caring and personable spirit. I learned so much from you and Mrs. Latner at the Glasscock School at Rice University.

Thank You, Gabby Bernstein for your upmost informational, motivational and inspirational Best Selling Masterclass.

Thank you, Rachelle, for your incalculable time and effort with making this happen. You are always a true friend to me.

Thank you, Tita and Dan. You went above and beyond for Jacob in the time of my and Raul's absence. Forever grateful and love you.

Thank you, April and Payo for always being there for me. Love You.

Thank you, Keri Bielitz, for being there every step of the way. You are my Forever Friend and Angel.

Thank You to all my friends at St. Cecilia: Kristine Fote, Angie Clinton, Kristi Hyzak, Stacey Hamilton and Teresa Ferruzzo. There are too many awesome friends to thank, you know who you are! Your forever love, support and friendship mean the world. Toni Giammalva and Vickie McCarthy, for your never-ending support and being forever friends throughout my long writing process. Your forever love, support, and friendship mean the world. Especially friends who supported TIRR via Maggie's Wonderful Pups, The Rexrode Family, The Greer Family, The Iglesias Family, The Hamilton Family, The Giammalva Family, The Powell Family and Susannah Hardesty Family. Thank you, Vickie Lovett Genietempo, for always supporting me and being my greatest cheerleader.

There are countless friends and family to mention. You know who you are. Thank you for making another chance possible for me, for helping me survive and come out of this with an unbroken mind.